Lorain County Community College
Library

Presented By

R. W. Beckett Corporation

In Honor Of

The LCCC Foundation

This collection of essays by celebrated authors centres on ideas of rationality and morality in economics. Recurrent themes are how to pursue and to model our acknowledged concern for others; and whether actual decision processes under uncertainty suggest standard theory needs to be revised: they are discussed from a wide range of perspectives, orthodox and radical, by a distinguished set of authors.

The contributors to the book are Frank Hahn, Amartya Sen, David Collard, Alan Ryan, Anthony Cramp, John Broome, Robin Matthews, and the editor, Gay Meeks.

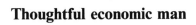

Thoughtful economic man

Thoughtful economic man

Essays on rationality, moral rules and benevolence

Edited by
J. Gay Tulip Meeks
Fellow of Robinson College, Cambridge

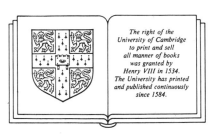

The right of the
University of Cambridge
to print and sell
all manner of books
was granted by
Henry VIII in 1534.
The University has printed
and published continuously
since 1584.

CAMBRIDGE UNIVERSITY PRESS
Cambridge
New York   Port Chester
Melbourne   Sydney

Published by the Press Syndicate of the University of Cambridge
The Pitt Building, Trumpington Street, Cambridge CB2 1RP
40 West 20th Street, New York, NY 10011, USA
10 Stamford Road, Oakleigh, Melbourne 3166, Australia

First published 1991

Printed in Great Britain at the University Press, Cambridge

British Library cataloguing in publication data
Thoughtful economic man: essays on rationality, moral rules and benevolence.
  1. Economics. Theories
  I. Meeks, J. Gay Tulip
  330.1

Library of Congress cataloguing information data
Thoughtful economic man: essays on rationality, moral rules and
benevolence/edited by J. Gay Tulip Meeks.
  p.   cm.
  Includes bibliographical references.
  ISBN 0 521 32574 9 (hardback)
  1. Economics – Moral and ethical aspects.   2. Decision-making.
3. Uncertainty.   4. Economic man.   I. Meeks, J. Gay Tulip.
HB72.T56   1991
330. 1 – dc20   90–1900
                   CIP

ISBN 0 521 32574 9 hardback

330.1
T524

VN

Contents

Preface

The origin of this book is the graduate course on philosophical issues in economics which I teach as part of the programme for the degree of M.Phil. in Economics at the University of Cambridge. I started to organise a series of seminars for this fairly novel course in 1980 and was somewhat surprised but very pleased both by the enthusiasm of its members and by the willingness of famous men to come and speak about questions of economic rationality and morality. It then seemed appropriate that their contributions should reach a wider audience; and so this collection of essays began.

It began some years ago. I am very grateful to the authors for their participation but even more grateful for their amazing patience with this most tardy editor: it is fortunate that the subjects of their papers are relatively timeless (the majority were actually written in 1985). Nearly all the essays were presented to the philosophical issues seminar at some stage and some have been kept in much their original form, with only minor changes; other essays were written specifically for publication; and so there is what I hope will be a refreshing variety of tone. My thanks are also due to those who have supported this interdisciplinary seminar series over the past decade, most particularly to the succession of very talented graduate students who have stimulated the whole project with their keen insight into the links between philosophy and economics.

Gay Meeks

Introduction

GAY MEEKS

This cluster of essays centres on ideas of rationality and morality in economics. Rational economic man has sometimes been very narrowly conceived as a crudely calculating self-interested maximiser. That this does less than justice to the scope of his motivations, the subtleties and boundaries of his processes of thought and the complexities of the decision situations that confront him will be a recurrent theme. Most of the essays in some way make a plea for greater richness and examine the implications of it: of allowing a due role for regard for others in society, for instance (whether in the form of benevolent motivation, altruistic rules, the demands of justice or Christian principle); or of incorporating awareness of the possible range of reasonable methods of decision under uncertainty. But there is much less agreement among the authors over whether the practical wisdom of this thoughtful economic man[1] fits happily into the orthodox model of rational choice, properly understood – sophisticated as to motive and to mind – or whether a radical upheaval in economic analysis is needed to accommodate him.

Hahn kicks off in essay 1 with a defence of the standard model of choice against Sen's well-known criticism that a 'rational' agent who attempts to express all the dimensions of his reasons for action just in a single utility ranking 'must be a bit of a fool'. Not so, says Hahn, for our preference ranking does achieve precisely that: competing motives, be they significant as they may, must still at the end of the day be traded against each other to yield a consistent ordering that can issue in rational action. It is a matter of having 'an integrated personality: a man knows what he wants'. But not all preferences will be self-interested ones and the rest of Hahn's essay asks how rational

---

[1] Patrick McCartan of Cambridge University Press has pointed out a possible feminist objection to this (title) phrase; so I hasten to add that 'man' is of course used here in the sense that is opposed to 'monkey', not to 'woman'. I hope this usage is as inoffensive as that which has drakes living on a duckpond.

economic agents can most effectively give substance to their concern for others. Benevolence aimed at particular people may act perversely on the general good;[2] yet an individual's attempts at 'anonymous' benevolence may be thwarted by his limited knowledge and by dependence of the outcome on what other agents do. Hahn concludes that, whether through Government or charities, 'actions for the "common good" . . . are best taken in common'.

Sen was invited to respond to Hahn; and the 'rational fool' complaint promptly resurfaces in essay 2. Here Sen replies that his quarrel was not with the idea of expressing a person's final choice between alternatives by means of a systematic preference ordering but rather with the practice of taking that ordering automatically to represent self-interest maximisation too – which would eliminate recognition of the variety of motivation that can underlie actual choice. As to the best means of putting benevolent motives into practice, Sen seconds the interest of the question but suggests there is unlikely to be a 'simple, qualitative answer' to it. Both particularised and 'anonymous' benevolence *can* succeed in being helpful: whether they actually do 'will depend on particular circumstances'.

The importance of particular circumstances is a central element in essay 3, where Collard analyses why in general 'love is not enough' to secure morally good results in economic life: typically altruistic sympathies will need to be accompanied both by a suitable ethical rule (to secure cooperative action) and by adequate knowledge (to show what the outcome of action is likely to be): 'we expect Love, Ethics and Reason'. In considering the ethics element, he investigates the constructive role of the Kantian imperatives, categorical and hypothetical, and the effect of an additional assumption about the duty to pay a fair share. It is then the 'reason' requirement, Collard argues, that 'perhaps surprisingly . . . provides the most difficulty': for – unless categorical moral duties can be invoked – the usual altruist with 'meddlesome' preferences seems to require some very complex and specific information, on appropriate macro modelling if that exists for instance, before he can be confident that each of his acts will indeed help others in the way that he intends. Four detailed cases are used to illustrate the problem. Yet for several reasons Collard remains more hopeful than was Hahn about the possibility of individual (but Kantian rule-following) altruists learning enough to

---

[2] Hahn refers here to an example in Matthews (1981). In that paper Matthews goes on to explore ways of identifying circumstances in which the general outcome is likely to be beneficial or perverse, complementing the discussion in the early essays here.

succeed in using market transactions as well as extra-market redistribution to achieve 'something positive' for others on *balance*, over the longer term, so that acting from altruistic principle would yield benefit as a general strategy.

In Ryan's paper (essay 4), the theme of regard for others is approached from the opposite direction: he focuses rather on the *lack* of it, for his topic is Marx's account of exploitation. He asks whether Marx can adequately be interpreted as simply protesting about the results of the interplay of rational self-interest under an (unjust) capitalist system of property rights and argues that he cannot: Marx's treatment is altogether different – he wants the abolition of property, not its mere reform – and the very notions of justice in exchange, of property rights and indeed of the rationality of orthodox calculating economic man are for him social products of the ('recent and local') capitalist mode of production itself. Ryan insists that Marx's analysis of exploitation has to be seen in holistic, not individualistic, terms – because it is part and parcel of the theory of value – and that there is therefore here 'a genuine parting of the ways between the research programme based on orthodox rational man analysis . . . and Marxism'. Which is then to be preferred? Ryan goes on to show why, if it has to be the former (and he rather thinks it has), the costs of that choice are high as Marx's attractively coherent account of exploitation is relinquished in favour of a property rights based approach – informed perhaps by Rawls or Nozick or Hayek – that, drawing on 'numerous intuitive notions about justice and ownership' and appealing variously to considerations of equality, efficiency, freedom and luck, soon 'run[s] into tensions' and can offer only a 'piecemeal explanation'.

But the paper that follows contends that Marxism is not the only unified alternative to the predominant model of rational man. Cramp notes in essay 5 the difficulty non-Marxian economists often seem to share in framing acceptable ethical principles capable of giving practical guidance, to fill the theoretical gap or (as he sees it) behaviourist vacuum left once the idea that own-utility-maximisation is the only basis for action is abandoned;[3] and he goes on to suggest that the problem could be overcome by the adoption of an economics 'congruent with Christian moral philosophy'. It is perhaps a curious comment on the boundaries of standard economics that the unfamiliar Christian perspective on economics which he champions tends to

---

[3] A difficulty suggested also in Sugden's (1984) description of the economic analysis of non-selfish behaviour as a 'particularly puzzling area' (p. 784).

be regarded as more unorthodox than the Marxian option itself, even though it might be held to be more in keeping with the traditional political and moral values of Western society. Cramp attacks the narrowness of some current versions of the Benthamite model by putting them in historical perspective; questions strict individualism, echoing Marx and Giddens on the dominance of production and on social influences on preference formation; accords with Sen on the possibility of 'sacrificial' behaviour; and responds to Schelling's discussion of competing motives and self-command by introducing arguments of St Paul and Kant to the effect that man is morally free to resist unworthy preferences, that reason can be judged to be on the side of conscience and thus that 'rational action is something to be achieved by struggling against desires, rather than by yielding to them'. This leads to a relatively optimistic conception of economic man as a meaningful agent, able to choose to act in accordance with principle and therefore (like Collard's *categorical* imperative Kantians) less troubled by the thorny problem of guessing consequences. Action based on the Christian norm of stewardship, Cramp goes on to explain, has radical implications both of only 'limited jurisdiction' over resources and of social responsibility for their use. Assessing the extent of 'stewardly surplus' would involve discounting apparent profit that arises from the exploitation of natural resources in excess,[4] of market power or of the labour force (through the violation of non-economic norms concerning regard for others). Yet, if conditions of work are not exploitative, work itself would be viewed as bringing fulfilment, not the disutility of standard analysis: this economic man sees wisdom in putting a positive value on employment.

The last three essays move away from economic morality and the question of how thoughtful economic man can make his caring for others effective, but continue the theme of economic rationality with its questions about his ways of thinking.

Broome in essay 6 defends the orthodox approach to rationality – expected utility theory, expressed in a careful form – against the doubts raised about its requirement of coherent preferences by apparent counter-examples to the sure-thing principle for decisions involving uncertainty. The counter-examples, ranging from Allais' to Diamond's, all invoke preferences claimed to be rational, yet which seem to breach the sure-thing principle: however, Broome argues that in justifying the preferences critics of the principle are in effect

---

[4] Offering one possible basis, then, for a 'green' economics.

revealing previously hidden differences between possibilities, differences which mean that the principle is not in fact being violated after all. Too coarse a scheme of individuation of possibilities can leave the sure-thing principle looking vulnerable, then, as the presentation of it has often tended to do; but both the sensation of doubt and the solution to it come from using a subtler one (that takes account, for instance, of feelings of disappointment or regret, or considerations of fair treatment of others, as well as material outcomes). Too *fine* a scheme of individuation, on the other hand, puts coherence at risk for another reason, threatening in the limit to make both the sure-thing principle and the axiom of transitivity ineffective in constraining practical preferences at all. So Broome augments the standard approach to rationality by introducing and defending a non-arbitrary way of deciding how finely to individuate possibilities, so as to give the familiar coherence requirements just the right force – enough to make them bite, but not so much as to undermine their appeal to reason. His proposal does put another axiom in doubt – Savage's first axiom of completeness of preferences among gambles – but Broome suggests that this axiom was in any case insecure and is best avoided by adopting a theory of expected utility, such as Jeffrey's, that does not rely on it.

The possibility that some apparent irrationalities might be regarded as rational once people's objectives are sufficiently carefully identified (including avoidance of regret in the utility function, say) also enters into essay 7, which reprints Matthews' 1984 Keynes Lecture to the British Academy. Matthews analyses the Keynesian idea that the motive for economic action in conditions of uncertainty arises in part not from its prospective consequences but from sheer animal spirits, from 'doing as well as having', so that the goals of the rational agent may be seen as including activity as an end in itself. After describing the Cambridge tradition of linking animal spirits with the response to uncertainty, he discusses how more recent thinking on the psychology of economic behaviour bears on each of them. On motivation, although the psychological literature does not offer an agreed theory, there turns out to be fair support for the activity idea, especially in respect of activity towards a self-selected target. On the cognitive side, a considerable body of evidence suggests that our rationality is limited not only by being bounded but also by being in some ways 'twisted' too, exhibiting systematic errors (though apparent cognitive failings may of course disappear if objectives are redefined, or may be functional in some way and thus 'serve a higher rationality', or may be concomitants of 'modes of thought that *in general* lead to better results than alternative ones'). Potentially, says Matthews, 'these are ideas with some radical and far-reaching implications for economics' and he outlines some economic phenomena in which the animal spirits factor may well be significant. His conclusion is that the psychological forces he has been considering – captured only in part by the animal spirits term – deserve more attention than conventional theory gives them but should not be tied so exclusively to the stimulus to invest in physical capital as Keynes himself seemed to propose: their effect might equally be felt in takeover behaviour, in investment in human capital or in developing new products or processes, or in many other non-routine economic activities.

The eighth and last essay in the book (my contribution) discusses the account Keynes gives of decision procedures under uncertainty and of the investment decision in particular, suggesting that his economically radical analysis is yet set in a respectable philosophical tradition. I think Keynes owes much to Hume in his approach to (inescapable) decision-making, in the face of a future that cannot be rationally known, as a blend of convention and animal spirits; although there is more to investment uncertainty than just inductive doubt and, again, Keynes goes rather further than Hume in his insistence that in behaving in this way we are doing the best we can in our uncomfortable cognitive circumstances – so that our actions can be counted reasonable, even rational, in a sense orthodox economic theory neglects. But Keynes' argument for viewing such behaviour as rational is at times confusing, even apparently inconsistent: the essay tries to separate out and assess the various elements in it, for the rationality claim is important – it is after all because the individual actions of investors are held to be rationally defensible yet capable of being collectively disastrous that Keynes sees so strong a need for intervention by the state.

In the volume, then, common themes; but a very wide range of perspectives.

References

Matthews, R.C.O. (1981), 'Morality, Competition and Efficiency', *The Manchester School*, 49: 289–309.
Sugden, R. (1984), 'Reciprocity: the Supply of Public Goods through Voluntary Contributions', *The Economic Journal*, 94: 772–87.

1   Benevolence

FRANK HAHN

It has been argued that the disposition to benevolence is scarce and that sensible societies have institutions which economise in the demands which they make on this disposition in the private actions of individuals. Matthews (1981) lists three reasons in support of this view: benevolence is not a reliable disposition, its object is rarely anonymous and it is limited by ignorance. There are other supporting arguments and one will want to look at these three with some care. There are also counter arguments such that benevolence must be practised if it is to survive as a propensity. But first I shall take a detour.

In *The Theory of Moral Sentiments* Adam Smith writes: 'How selfish soever man may be supposed, there are evidently some principles in his nature, which interest him in the fortune of others, and render their happiness necessary to him, though he derives nothing from it except the pleasure of seeing it' (1976, p. 9). This principle in man's nature which no doubt is a true principle, may be thought to negate the doctrine of the Invisible Hand.

Smith however does not deny selfishness. Not only does he say 'how selfish soever,' etc., but he also writes that the benevolent man 'gets nothing from it' but adds 'except the pleasure of seeing it'. This seems to rule out benevolence the fruits of which cannot be observed (or at best imagined) and that is important in thinking about the principle. Certainly there is nothing in this passage which needs to call forth objections from a Benthamite.

Now Amartya Sen in a paper called 'Rational Fools' wants to take matters rather further. We understand sentences like 'he sacrificed his happiness for another' and our understanding comes, so Sen argues, from the recognition that people's actions are guided by a variety of motives. Some of these are purely self-directed while others concern outsiders etc. For instance, the traditional motive which is supposed to power the Invisible Hand is only one amongst many. Clearly Sen is correct at a level of analysis which concerns states of mind. But I think he has confused others, especially non-economists, when it comes to action. Why do you give the beggar ten pence and not ten pounds? Why do you visit your friend in hospital once a week and not daily? You are evidently trading between competing desires and motives. But trades involve comparisons and comparisons require comparability. This can be achieved in thinking of the individual not as in search of happiness, or respectability or physical well being but as having preferences over a suitable domain of alternatives. This essentially becomes a theory of the integrated personality: a man knows what he wants.

What he wants, Social Biology and Selfish Genes notwithstanding, is no doubt the outcome of social and personal environment. But the history of Christianity and of the Cultural Revolution suggests that preferences cannot be changed easily or rapidly and that giving weight to the welfare of anonymous others is not a general feature. Indeed, while no doubt there are notable pitfalls in believing this, I am surprised how much we seem to understand the actions of people in the remote past. This in turn suggests at least a certain degree of stability in preferences. It certainly seems safe to aver that at all times a relevant description of the domain of choice includes the welfare or ill-fare of some other persons; this is simply to aver that we live in society. The interesting question is not: 'Do we care about others?' but, 'How much do we care and for which others?'. The not unimportant further point is that to be rational does not entail being greedy or being Ruskin's one-dimensional economic man.

I can now turn to the main argument. I begin by noting that benevolence need not imply that one weighs the interests or happiness of others: it may be purely instrumental. The institution of reciprocal gifts in some tribal societies is one example. There is also the interesting view that this may be a general feature of most societies. My altruistic behaviour is occasioned by the risk that I may myself be in need of altruism and that it will not be forthcoming if I had acted differently. Indeed if one thinks about it one can cast an argument from Imaginative Sympathy in this form. Doing so would allow an explanation of benevolent acts without invoking Smith's principle.

But while there is something in this purely instrumental view it is plainly too extreme to be applied to benevolence in general. Adam Smith's principle seems to me to have great force in what I shall call 'named benevolence'. By this I mean benevolent acts which arise from the welfare of other named individuals being in the domain of my preferences. 'Friends before Country' is an example of named benevolence as is Nepotism and gifts to one's children. Contrary to some American writers I am willing to grant that such benevolence is not purely instrumental. There is, of course, a gradation from named to anonymous benevolence, that is from one's family, to one's friends, to colleagues, to town, to country, etc. It is part of most economists' contention that, instrumental benevolence excepted, most benevolence is pretty close to named benevolence.

And how could it be otherwise? To love everyone equally means to love no-one at all. But it is equally important that we do not know how to act in the interest of anonymous benevolence. Consider a firm with an unprofitable factory which it has the means to keep going. If it closes down it harms the workers it knows. If it does not it is likely to harm workers and other people it does not know. It is not reasonable to suppose that a private agent can perform the required calculations. Moreover, and of rather central significance, even if he could calculate, the outcome would depend on the benevolence of others. In fact anonymous benevolence is in the nature of a public good. That is so because the state in which I find others will depend on how far the benevolence of others has already operated and the fruitfulness of my own benevolence is likely to be affected by this. So even if one neglects the argument from ignorance it is unlikely that the operation of anonymous benevolence will lead to a quantum of such benevolence which would be chosen if we all acted cooperatively.

But if it is hard to see what it is we ask of people when we ask them to act in the interest of anonymous benevolence it must now also be noted that it is not clearly desirable that they should display benevolence closer to the named variety. I have already mentioned such obvious evils as Nepotism. But there are less obvious examples. Here is one given by Matthews.

British firms in South Africa have been urged to pay their black workers more and treat them better than is generally the case there. Of course there is an argument of setting a good example. But why should these firms be urged to act benevolently specifically in regard to *their* workers? Would it not be better if they spent money on schools, health centres or black agitation? Indeed is it clear that if they are to sacrifice profits it would not be better to take on more workers at the prevailing conditions? By 'better' I mean that it serves the purposes of anonymous benevolence. I use that expression because I hold the view that moral injunctions cannot be named injunctions.

The argument then suggests that we should make matters of anonymous benevolence the subject of actions taken collectively or of rules designed collectively and that it is likely that in asking benevolence to play a major role in private action we would either not be understood, or if understood would induce bad outcomes. To ask firms to act with 'Social Responsibility' is not to ask them anything comprehensible and at best will lead to particularised benevolence which harms the common good. Exactly the same would apply to workers' cooperatives or to Unions. Adam Smith proposed that the operation of private preference including amongst these the weight given to named benevolence, provided it was constrained by competition and a relatively small degree of public morality would render private dispositions least harmful to the common good. It would of course be wrong to suppose that this arrangement would also lead to that degree of anonymous benevolence which we jointly might regard as proper. In the basic contention however it seems to me that a further two hundred years of thought on the matter have supported Smith. There simply is no other credible way to decentralise decisions.

The argument which I have advanced is that actions for the 'common good', that is actions designed to further the project of anonymous benevolence, are best taken in common and that it is neither feasible, nor, if it were, desirable to make anonymous benevolence the mainspring of private decisions. It is important here to stress that it is not only the limited capacity for benevolence which we possess – the scarcity aspect – which leads to this conclusion, although it supports it. At least as important is the argument from efficiency and lucidity. That is there will be more to allocate to benevolent purposes if (anonymous) benevolence is not a mainspring of private decisions and the motive of (anonymous) benevolence can be given concrete interpretation if it is part of cooperative decision procedures.

To this view there are several objections. One of these is that a society in which the private actions of individuals are informed only by private concerns (including the concern of named benevolence) is not one in which individuals can realise their full moral potential. The pursuit of private interests is regarded as base and to act for the common good as noble. Moreover benevolence which is not individually practised will wither altogether. This objection has some merit but it can be met by what I have argued is the desirable procedure.

If anonymous benevolence is to be the subject of cooperative action then it will require a disposition to cooperate for this purpose. For instance one agrees to be taxed and does not cheat the tax man. Thus while I argue for a separation of the domains of choice into private and public I have not proposed that there be no public discussion at all. Nor is it required that the 'public' be interpreted as entirely in the sphere of Government. Adequate cooperation may be achieved by charitable organisations. There is nothing here to lead to the withering of the propensity for anonymous benevolence. When I help a distressed aunt or when I decide how much to invest considerations of the public good should, for reasons which I have given, not intervene. This however does not entail that I should take no actions for the public good.

References

Matthews, R.C.O. (1981), 'Morality, Competition and Efficiency', *The Manchester School*, 49: 289–309.

Sen, A.K. (1977), 'Rational Fools: A Critique of the Behavioural Foundations of Economic Theory', *Philosophy and Public Affairs*, 6: 317–44, reprinted in H. Harris (ed.) (1978), *Scientific Models and Man*, Oxford: Clarendon Press; F.H. Hahn and M. Hollis (eds.) (1979), *Philosophy and Economic Theory*, Oxford: Clarendon Press; A.K. Sen (1982), *Choice, Welfare and Measurement*, Oxford: Basil Blackwell, and Cambridge, Mass.: MIT Press.

Smith, A. (1976), *The Theory of Moral Sentiments* (first published 1759), edited by D.D. Raphael and A.L. Macfie, Oxford: Clarendon Press, Glasgow Edition of the *Works and Correspondence of Adam Smith*, Vol. I.

2 Beneconfusion

AMARTYA SEN

Frank Hahn's interesting essay on 'Benevolence'[1] starts off with the worry that my paper 'Rational Fools',[2] while 'correct' at some level, has in fact 'confused others, especially non-economists, when it comes to action'. On reading Hahn's paper, I realise that I might possibly have confused an economist as well. Confusions can, of course, be beneficial in some circumstances, and I am pleased that Hahn's decision to dispute what he takes to be my contentions has given us the opportunity to read his ideas on as important a subject as benevolence. I agree with many things he says, but I shall concentrate, in this brief reply, on things on which we seem to differ. I am sure that Frank Hahn would never forgive me if I did not dwell on our differences.

Integration and distinction

Hahn picks for critical examination one particular point from my paper 'Rational Fools', to wit, as Hahn puts it, 'that people's actions are guided by a variety of motives' and that 'some of these are purely self-directed while others concern outsiders etc'.[3] Hahn is right to note that the existence of such a variety of motives does not entail that the person must lack an 'integrated personality', and that it is indeed possible to think of 'the individual not as in search of happiness, or respectability, or physical well-being, but as having preferences over a suitable domain of alternatives'.[4] This seems to me to be just right, and not at all in conflict with anything I said in the paper under discussion.

What then is the problem? It is important to distinguish between two quite different issues, to wit: (1) whether people do typically have

---

[1] See above, p. 7.   [2] Sen (1977).   [3] See above, p. 7.   [4] *Ibid.*, p. 8.

integrated personalities, and (2) whether an integrated person's preferences can be seen in terms of his or her self-interest. As a matter of fact, I have less confidence than Hahn has that (as he puts it) 'a man knows what he wants', but that question, and more generally, issue (1), were not the subject of the theses presented in my paper, which was primarily concerned with issue (2). The different and possibly conflicting *interpretations* of what is often – rather confusingly – called by the same name, viz., 'the preference ordering' of a person, was indeed a central concern of my paper. The point related to the fact that a lot of economic theory takes a 'preference ordering' to represent many *different* things, including *inter alia* the person's self-interest *and* also his or her basis for choice, and these need not, in general, coincide.

For example, in standard 'general equilibrium theory', well presented by, say, Arrow and Hahn,[5] the preference ordering of a person represents both (1) the basis of each individual's *choices* (indeed the proofs of the *existence* of general equilibrium depend on this characterisation), and (2) the person's *self-interest* or *individual well-being*, which is taken as the basis of judging what competitive market equilibria achieve (e.g. *Pareto optimality*). The issue raised in 'Rational Fools' was not whether each of these rankings might not be nicely ordered and well-integrated (indeed both self-interest and choice may well be neatly structured), but whether the *same* ordering could, in general, represent *both*. In the context of the theses presented in 'Rational Fools', Hahn's pointer to the possibility that 'a man knows what he wants' would seem to be a red herring.

In 'Rational Fools' the chief thesis was presented in the following terms:

If our argument so far has been correct . . . traditional theory has *too little* structure. A person is given *one* preference ordering, and as and when the need arises this is supposed to reflect his interests, represent his welfare, summarize his idea of what should be done, and describe his actual choices and behaviour. Can one preference ordering do all these things? A person thus described may be 'rational' in the limited sense of revealing no inconsistencies in his choice behaviour, but if he has no use for these distinctions between quite distinct concepts, he must be a bit of a fool. . . . Economic theory has been much preoccupied with this rational fool bedecked in the glory of his *one* all-purpose preference ordering.[6]

[5] Arrow and Hahn (1971).
[6] Sen (1977). In Hahn and Hollis (1979), p. 102 and in Sen (1982), p. 99. See also Sen (1987).

The point to note here is that the critique is *not* concerned with disputing that a person's choices may be based on an integrated personality, or with arguing that the choice function representing the person's actual behaviour may fail to be binary and ordinal. It was concerned with disputing that a person's *choice ordering* (i.e. the ordering relation underlying the person's choice function) can be invariably interpreted as the person's *self-interest* or *individual welfare*. This is precisely where the existence of a 'variety of motives' makes a difference. A person who chooses on the basis of a systematic preference ordering that takes note of self-interest as well as other objectives may well possess an integrated personality, but his or her behaviour would not typically coincide with one of self-interest maximisation. The opposite of a 'rational fool' is not an unintegrated person.

Costs and benefits of benevolence

Frank Hahn also goes into the advantages and disadvantages of benevolent behaviour. This issue is, of course, a different one still.

Here Hahn seems to have a big problem with accepting that benevolence can be beneficial. On the one hand, he believes that 'it is part of most economists' contention that instrumental behaviour excepted, most benevolence is pretty close to *named* benevolence',[7] i.e. benevolence not directed at *all* others, but at some named individuals. On the other hand, he explains that he uses the word 'better' to 'mean that it serves the purposes of anonymous benevolence', because he holds 'the view that moral injunctions cannot be named injunctions'.[8] The claims of 'anonymous benevolence' may 'not be understood' and may indeed be, in Frank Hahn's view, ununderstandable, and the pursuit of 'named benevolence' may make matters worse from a moral point of view. Hahn illustrates the dilemma with the remark that 'to ask firms to act with "Social Responsibility" is not to ask them anything comprehensible and at best will lead to particularised benevolence which harms the common good.'[9]

An impasse here? Hahn is clearly bothered by the fact that moral judgements may require universalisation of some kind, and this would seem to conflict with benevolence towards some particular

---

[7] See above, p. 9; italics added.   [8] *Ibid.*, pp. 9–10.   [9] *Ibid.*, p. 10.

individuals, which is the form that benevolence is most likely to take. He seems to overlook the simple fact that universalisation admits the use of general parameters that in specific contexts will take a 'named' form. That is indeed a part of the characterisation of universalisation that has been noted by authors as diverse as Immanuel Kant, Henry Sidgwick, John Rawls, Richard Hare and John Mackie, to name just a few.[10] 'Love thy neighbour' may be a good *general* principle, which produces benefits for all and sundry, but in acting according to that general principle, the neighbours loved must have particular identities. You have to *identify* your neighbours before you love them.

There is no real impasse in recommending benevolence of the kind that seems to worry Hahn. This does not, however, necessarily disestablish his main contention: 'The argument which I have advanced is that actions for the "common good", that is actions designed to further the project of anonymous benevolence, are best taken in common and that it is neither feasible, nor, if it were, desirable to make anonymous benevolence the mainspring of private decisions.'[11] That contention would require a more specific scrutiny – something that Hahn does not provide and one which I am not about to attempt here.

We should be grateful to Frank Hahn for raising interesting and important questions as to what benevolence does or does not do. His belief that he is somehow correcting confusions generated in my paper seems ungrounded, and his own confused interpretation of the main contentions of that paper may not contribute much to clarity. But, at the same time, the fact that Hahn does address questions about the place and role of benevolence in economic and social matters is an entirely beneficial outcome. His analysis provides a welcome contrast with the increasingly narrow concentration of modern economics.

I should, finally, end with a rather elementary point. The parameterised form of universalisation will often take us, as discussed above, to particular persons with specific identities. It was discussed why there is nothing odd about this general–particular relationship. But sometimes the concrete applications of general principles may not, in fact, make the identities of the beneficiaries clear, and still the actions in favour of the general interest can be

---

[10] Perhaps the most extensive discussion of this issue is to be found in Mackie (1977), chapter 4 ('Universalization').   [11] See above, p. 10.

beneficial and far from 'harmful'. For example, we may not know exactly *who* will live in the future, but long-run actions to protect the environment may still do a lot more good than disregarding the interests of *unknown* people in the future.

Benevolence may help, or may not. That will depend on particular circumstances. But there is no *general* presumption against benevolence: neither against '*named* benevolence', nor against '*anonymous* benevolence'. Frank Hahn's question as to which types of benevolence are helpful and which harmful is one of very considerable interest, but the kind of simple qualitative answer he seeks has, for reasons discussed, little plausibility. Practical reason over such complex domains clearly must take a more contingent form. That, at any rate, should not come as a surprise.

References

Arrow, K.J. and Hahn, F.H. (1971), *General Competitive Analysis*, San Francisco: Holden-Day.

Hahn, F.H. (1990), 'Benevolence', essay 1 in this volume.

Mackie, J. (1977), *Ethics*, Harmondsworth: Penguin Books.

Sen, A.K. (1977), 'Rational Fools: A Critique of the Behavioural Foundations of Economic Theory', *Philosophy and Public Affairs*, 6: 317–44; reprinted in H. Harris (ed.) (1978), *Scientific Models and Man*, Oxford: Clarendon Press; F.H. Hahn and M. Hollis (eds.) (1979), *Philosophy and Economic Theory*, Oxford: Clarendon Press; A.K. Sen (1982), *Choice, Welfare and Measurement*, Oxford: Basil Blackwell, and Cambridge, Mass.: MIT Press.

(1987), *On Ethics and Economics*, Oxford: Basil Blackwell.

3 Love is not enough*

DAVID COLLARD

I

Though the theme of this paper is, indeed, that 'love is not enough' it may very well be that it is sometimes too much. There then arises what I like to call the after-you problem: each gives priority to the other, nothing gets done, all are worse off. Even this extreme case has its use in illustrating the main point that I wish to make, for the after-you problem is in practice usually solved rather quickly. If only one piece of chocolate is left we share it or toss for it. If there is a jam in the doorway one of us passes through after a ritual of embarrassed politeness. The actors surely perceive in such cases that a thorough-going after-you solution would be Pareto-inferior and take steps, as it were, to avoid it. At the heart of the matter lie the actors' perceptions of the 'true' model.

Briefly my argument is that altruism, or something very like it, is a pre-condition of moral economic behaviour: but that, although it is necessary, it is certainly not sufficient. Knowledge of the correct underlying model also seems to be necessary. This is a very stiff requirement, however, so while the essay is mainly concerned with the Kantian Hypothetical Imperative it has some recourse to the less contingent Categorical Imperative.

I need first to recall some of the main points from my *Altruism and Economy* (1978, 1981). I argued in the book that instances of apparent altruism (voluntary giving, helping behaviour, etc.) were so widespread that it was just as well to put concern for others into the utility function as to adopt a series of *ad hoc* extensions of self-interest. It is not clear, however, whether altruism should be treated as a scarce resource to be economised upon (as Robertson had

* I am grateful to participants in the Cambridge Seminar for their comments at the time and to Gay Meeks for helpful comments on a first draft.

suggested) or as a faculty which, like muscle power, develops through use. I inclined, and still incline, to the latter, more hopeful, view.

Much depended on whether preferences were 'meddlesome' or 'non-meddlesome'. Meddlesome preferences are those which are concerned with the composition of the consumption of others: non-meddlesome preferences are concerned only with their 'utilities'. One dramatic but intuitively acceptable conclusion was that, with non-meddlesome preferences, altruism simply lops the ends off the contract locus without causing it to 'twist'. Less technically it is perfectly acceptable to behave in what Wicksteed called a 'non-tuistic' fashion whereby redistributive actions and market transactions are kept in separate compartments. There is no inconsistency in the altruist buying in the cheapest market and selling in the dearest, provided he carries out extra-market redistribution. Love doesn't matter: the conditions for efficient production and exchange are unaffected.

But the non-meddlesome case is a rather unusual one. Our concern is, in practice, almost always rather specific: for example, that others do not go hungry or badly housed. It is often thought that meddlesomeness is an inconsistent characteristic of altrusim. I cannot see that this is so. It is true that generally, though not always, recipients would prefer equivalent extra income to extra benefits. But we cannot observe their utilities: they do not wear utility meters on their faces. And we do know from our own experience that minimum levels of mobility, warmth, food, etc., are essential to decent life. So it is hardly surprising that an altruist, whose preferences very much arise from sympathetic identification, should wish for specific rather than general redistribution. Once meddlesomeness is admitted the old efficiency conditions will no longer do and some restrictions on trading, or taxes and subsidies, are in order. Love does matter after all.

Sometimes, and this is our central concern, love does matter but turns out not to be enough. In the well-known Prisoners' Dilemma selfish individuals pursuing their own interests are held, by an invisible band, in a Pareto-inferior outcome. It is easy to show that in an n person Prisoner's Dilemma the individual will be tempted to free-ride even if he attaches some altruistic weight to other people's pay-offs. In games with just a few players the position is rather easier and in repeated two-person games the players seem to find mutual accommodation rather easily. In such small games a combination of love and trust may be sufficient. The great question is whether there are any ethical rules whereby individuals might bind themselves so as to produce good outcomes. It was shown in *Altruism and Economy* that there are, indeed, several such rules: for example, the Christian rule of turning the other cheek, rule Utilitarianism and the Kantian rule.

II

In illustrating the notion of the Kantian altruist I made use, in my book, of the much discussed case of blood-doning. The donor's utility function is taken to include, with positive first derivative, the probability (p) of an unknown Other being able to obtain blood if necessary. A Kantian rule is then applied: choose that action which would, if also taken by similarly motivated others, result in a good outcome. More colloquially, would it do if everybody behaved like me?[1] In the book the model was used to discuss the possible response of a voluntary donor to a mixed system. Consider a purely voluntary system. If I and similarly motivated others refuse to give, p will fall to zero as soon as current stocks are used up. Now consider a mixed system. This is rather harder to model. Suppose the authorities are interested in a high p. If I and similarly motivated others refuse to donate, the authorities will presumably induce a larger paid supply by raising price: whether they will succeed in doing so is something the potential voluntary donor will have to judge. If the authorities are successful p will not be affected by our withdrawal. So, in so far as willingness to give was grounded in an interest in p (and there could be powerful other inducements), there will be no reason why Kantian altruists should not withdraw.

I insist that, in explaining voluntary redistribution, altruistic motivation is just as essential as the Kantian rule. Sugden (1982) has suggested that the Kantian rule is sufficient. Here it is useful to distinguish between the categorical and the hypothetical imperatives. The categorical imperative (CI) is concerned with my inescapable

[1] It is sometimes objected that the Kantian rule is absurd: is it immoral for me to eat at a restaurant, given that if everyone tried to do so it would be impossible? The rule seems absurd because of the way in which the question is framed. Rather one should ask, 'is it immoral for me and people like me to eat at restaurants when we wish to and have the money?' The answer might well be 'yes' but the rule is not an absurd one.

moral duty as a human being: it dictates that there are certain things I must do, like saving a life when I can. The hypothetical imperative (HI) is much more contextual, for the rightness of the action depends on its expected outcome. There is a strong utilitarian element here. Most of the issues we have to deal with in the social sciences are to do with the hypothetical, not the categorical, imperative. Then it is obvious that the altruistic assumption is also required because, by itself, the Kantian rule is ends-neutral: we could behave Kantianly just as well for a bad end as for a good one.

Altruism (or sympathy or empathy) is not merely an ingredient of moral actions, it defines them. Without altruism no problem of moral conduct exists. This is a strong claim: let me defend it. The egotist faces an economic problem but not a moral one. Other people (and indeed the whole of the rest of creation) are purely instrumental. They do not need to be taken into account at all as ends. We may make no distinction between how the egotist behaves (in economic life) and how he ought to behave: his duty is to serve himself. Sometimes, admittedly, the means to his self-interest will be obscure, as is the case with the Prisoners' Dilemma, and he may make mistakes but on the whole there is a one-to-one correspondence between ends and means. The altruist, on the other hand, does have a moral problem: viz., given that I have such and such a concern for others how ought I to behave? And the (HI) Kantian rule is intended to provide just such guidance.

III

Because there are certain difficulties in the application of the rule it is worth noticing the many situations in which it is not at all necessary. Things are very much easier if the altruist operates on a small scale. Thus the (CI) Kantian will wish to treat all the other individuals with whom he or she has dealings as real persons, i.e., as ends rather than means. He will therefore not discriminate on grounds such as age, sex or race. And, like a good altruist should, he will rescue people from rivers, buses or crashed cars as required. (The CI–HI distinction cannot, of course, be rigidly maintained as even acts like life-saving often need a quick, rational, assessment of probabilities, etc.) These are all one-to-one relationships. Similarly with the (HI) Kantian who chooses to run local clubs for bored teenagers or playgroups or whatever. Here the public good is a very local one and the individual has no need to theorise about and attempt to model some distant outcome of his actions: it is there for all to see. The relationship is not quite one-to-one but it is one-to-a-few and the group is sufficiently small for the defection of one helper to be a serious event.

The rule is designed not for this type of case but for cases where there is a significant potential free-rider problem. The size of the group is obviously important and we need to say a little about it. So far I have assumed a group of 'like-minded' or 'similarly motivated' Kantian altruists. A sharp division of the population seems to be implied between those who 'care' enough to want to do something and the rest who take absolutely no interest. More realistically different people will be altruistically motivated to differing degrees. There is likely to be a continuum of concern, running from the deeply committed to the apathetic. Even the Kantian altruist will have to set costs against his own valuation of benefits to others.

This matter of group size may be made a little clearer by drawing upon the theory of clubs (see figure 3.1). Let some level of provision of public good be under consideration at a total cost of C. If n people share the cost, the cost per person is C/n as shown in the figure. Let each person value the provision at v and plot v in rank order of individual preference for provision. It is assumed that the v curve is less concave than the cost curve. This very simple apparatus may now be put to work in order to say something about the size of the relevant Kantian group.

(1) No Kantian group is possible below n^* as the shared cost is greater than anyone's willingness to pay. Obviously if $n^* > n$, where n is the total decision-taking population, there can be no Kantian group at all.

(2) A Kantian group of n^* will be adequate to provide the service required. Given that an enthusiastic group of n^* Kantians exists why should further Kantian altruists bother to join in sharing the costs? Up to n^* the usual Kantian generalisation leads to an obligation to join. But after this we need a further assumption to do with perceived fairness. This is that the Kantian altruist feels it to be his or her duty to pay a fair share of the cost of provision.

(3) With the additional assumption about fairness the Kantian group may be expected to rise to n^{**}. Notice that the area of net consumers' surplus is absolutely given once n^* have joined. After that it is only a matter of distribution.

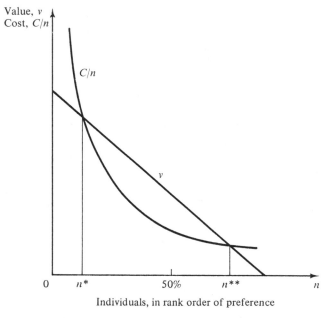

Figure 3.1

(4) Should n^{**} occur at above 50% of the electorate the enlarged
    Kantian group would be able, if it so wished, to force non-
    Kantians to share costs, thus now paying at a slightly lower rate
    themselves than before. Such a group would presumably feel that
    any unfairness towards those unwilling to contribute was more
    than offset by the provision itself and by fairness towards fellow
    Kantians.

Thus we have been able to make a little progress given some
simplifying assumptions. The size of the Kantian group will be n^*, or
n^{**} if the auxiliary assumption of fairness is added. At n^* the sub-
marginal (HI) Kantians are essentially free-riding, something that a
(CI) Kantian would never do.

IV

So far it has been taken for granted that the individual is pretty sure
what the results of his or her Kantian behaviour will be. It soon
becomes clear that we are, in fact, asking rather a lot. Consider the

ordinary individual wishing to behave morally in economic life. Three things are expected:

(1) altrusitic sympathies,
(2) an (HI) Kantian rule,
(3) knowledge of the outcome.

We expect Love, Ethics and Reason.

Perhaps surprisingly, it is this last which provides the most difficulty for it implies that the individual is capable of correctly modelling the whole situation, including the responses of markets and of other individuals. This comes very close to assuming an all-embracing version of 'rational expectations'. For some sorts of situation the rational expectations assumption is not a bad one to make. The dealer in an informed and efficient commodity market will, on the whole, make correct guesses about market price: farmers who should in theory be susceptible to price and output 'cobwebs' seem to locate the true equilibrium without too much trouble: players in a two-person repeated Prisoners' Dilemma perceive the illusory nature of the sucker and free-rider pay-offs . . . and so on. But it is impossible to accept rational expectations as a general assumption for the sorts of action we are now considering. It will, of course, commonly happen that we have strong feelings about issues (such as feeding the hungry, environmental pollution or racial discrimination) about which our technical knowledge is meagre. Unfortunately reason and knowledge are much more important than feelings at this stage of the argument. Strong feelings do not disqualify us from action: but they may cause us to do things which result in the opposite of what we had intended.

Clearly we need some sort of help for few would be able to carry through the 'practical reasoning' aspect of Kantian behaviour without guidance. One ludicrous solution would be to assign to anyone affected by sympathetic feelings a socio-economic modeller, rather in the manner that social workers may be assigned to those having difficulty in coping with more mundane economic life. More practically it would not be unreasonable to expect some guidance from the social sciences.

V

To illustrate some of the difficulties I have taken a few issues of economic morality. They are all complex issues on which one could write at length but the descriptions here are brief and stylised. I use them to draw out some common threads.

(i) A South African Boycott. The issue is whether or not I should boycott South African goods. My interest in the issue is that I wish to hasten the end of apartheid which I believe to be an evil system. It does not much matter, for the present purpose, whether I wish to end it because of a direct empathy with those discriminated against or because of a moral conviction that apartheid is wrong. The reason why it does not matter is that between my desired end and my required action stands the model, which has to incorporate some of the following features:

the costs to me (us) of buying possibly more expensive and/or inferior substitutes,
the effects of our actions on the real income of Coloureds, Blacks and Afrikaaners,
the effects of our actions on the morale and strength of anti-apartheid groups in South Africa and elsewhere,
the direct and indirect political consequences of the above.

It is not obvious that the effects will be those intended: the fact that I nevertheless wish to support a boycott is a matter to which I return.

(ii) Voluntary Overseas Aid. Suppose that I wish to prevent some of the poorest people in the world from starving. The issue is whether I should make a regular donation to War On Want or a similar charity. Again either the categorical imperative or 'altruism plus the hypothetical imperative' will do, but let us assume HI. And again the implied model has to include:

the direct and indirect costs of our contributions,
the efficiency of the organisation in ensuring that my contributions actually reach the poorest people (not simply the governments of poor countries),
the direct and indirect effects of the schemes adopted on incomes per head of the target groups and others, including effects on domestic food production,
the effects of our actions on donations by others, including official aid.

This last point is very close to the point made in the earlier blood-doning example. If the UK Government clearly stated that official aid would be so adjusted as to bring the total of voluntary and official aid together to 1% of GNP then the (HI) Kantian would have no incentive to give. The (CI) Kantian might still wish to do so.

(iii) Immunisation. The parent concerned only with his or her own children will need to know:

the immediate cost, including inconvenience, of the inoculation,
the effectiveness of the treatment against the occurrence of the relevant condition (e.g. whooping cough), depending partly on the degree of protection already afforded,
the likelihood and nature of undesirable side effects.

The parent who is concerned with other people's children as well will have to consider what might happen if a significant number of parents chose not to allow inoculation for their child. There is no reason why the non-Kantian should take this into account. Even when it is taken into account the parent might still decide, of course, not to allow treatment. Though this is a difficult decision to take it is not quite as complicated as the two earlier decisions as only a few simple pieces of additional information are required.

(iv) Miners' Families. (This was highly topical at the time of the seminar on which this paper is based. No doubt it will seem dated by now). Suppose that I am anxious to help the families of striking miners. The (HI) Kantian again needs to know several things:

the extent to which my (our) food contributions actually get to the families,
the effect of our contributions upon the attitudes of others towards the miners and on the morale of the mining communities,
the effect of our contributions on the duration of the strike,
the likelihood of the strike being successful.

If the (HI) Kantian believes that the strike will ultimately be unsuccessful and that his donations will probably increase its length, then he possibly ought not to contribute. Again, the (CI) Kantian may not feel so constrained.

VI

Some common threads run through these examples.
At several points it was observed that the (CI) case seemed to

present less difficulty than the (HI) case. This was so because (HI) actions are purely instrumental whereas (CI) actions are good in themselves. But this can only be so where the links between action and consequence are immediate and direct: otherwise some intervening model is required and we are back to the (HI) case. While it may be a good thing in itself to abolish apartheid or feed the hungry, the boycotting of South African goods or giving to War On Want cannot be seen in the same light: they are means, not ends.

In all of the examples it was necessary to talk in terms of the first person plural rather than the first person singular: this was because of the generalisation inherent in the Kantian rule. It is important to emphasise again that the Kantian rule does not eliminate the free-rider problem though it does change its character. To go back to the earlier simple model, it is the Kantian's duty to take part as long as his own valuation is above that of individual n^* whereas the non-Kantian, even the non-Kantian altruist, is unlikely to participate.

Some of the models require complex and controversial social science. For example the South African case requires a knowledge of the theory of international trade, the theory of income distribution and theories of political processes; the Aid case requires the theory of economic development (at least); the Immunisation case requires the theory of epidemiology and of risk; the Miners' case requires a theory of industrial relations (at least). It would be absurd to pretend that even the expert, let alone the ordinary individual, could have a working knowledge of all the relevant theory. So must our conclusion be that the Knowledge and Reason requirement for (HI) Kantian action is totally unrealistic?

If this is our conclusion it does, of course, leave the door wide open for a universal non-tuism. We do not know enough to decide whether any act of Kantian altruism will have the desired results. In the absence of such knowledge is it not better to leave well alone? By interfering we might well make matters worse. This feeling is strengthened by the economist's normal assumption of risk aversion in the face of uncertainty.

VII

Are matters really as bad as this for the potential do-gooder? Probably not. One valid, though rather weak, defence is that the zero option also has incalculable consequences, i.e. doing nothing is also risky. A second line of defence has to do with information. One of the major activities of voluntary organisations is the dissemination of information and reassurance. Many of them produce leaflets or newsletters or advertisements to tell subscribers how their money is being spent. These reports, particularly of the larger organisations, are widely discussed and criticised in the media. There is therefore something analogous to an open market in information. Though highly imperfect (the entrepreneurs concerned will sometimes wish to embroider the truth) and only roughly analogous, it is probably not a great deal less satisfactory than the market in information associated with most consumer durables. The difference, of course, is that it is a great deal less easy to 'test' allegations about the effectiveness of donations to an anti-apartheid campaign than it is to test allegations about the effectiveness of a washing machine.

A second line of defence is that many of the socio-economic models which would, in principle, give us guidance (could we but comprehend them) are, in any case, not very satisfactory. They are not always able to give concrete predictions about the effects of specific actions. People have then to rely on much broader and cruder indications of what might happen. They might very well reason in an intuitive fashion that they are likely to do good if, in general and over the long term, they give their support and encouragement to proposals to help the disadvantaged, the discriminated against, the poor, the ill and so on: that they will make mistakes but that (Kantianly though not necessarily individually) they will achieve something positive. This line of defence suggests that my Kantian model is much too tactical in nature leaving out longer term, more general, strategic considerations.

The theme of this paper has been that 'love is not enough'. It is often unnecessary (the non-twisting theorem) and hardly ever sufficient. The great building blocks of moral behaviour in economic life are Sympathy, Morality and Practical Reason. It is the task of social scientists, not of moral philosophers, to provide the last of these. To the extent that their models are defective the Kantian altruist (whilst not being endowed with rational expectations) must continue to rely heavily on his or her intuition. But in the heavily populated middle ground of economic morality, between the spontaneity of personal contact and the grandeur of meta-morality, there is room for the economist to enlarge the possibility of successful moral conduct in economic life.

References

Collard, D.A. (1978), *Altruism and Economy*, Oxford: Martin Robertson.
(1983), 'Economics of Philanthropy: a Comment', *Economic Journal*, 93: 637–8.

Sugden, R. (1982), 'On the Economics of Philanthropy', *Economic Journal*, 92: 341–50.

4 Exploitation, justice, and the rational man

ALAN RYAN

This essay is devoted to three contentious issues, and it is deliberately contentious about all of them. The contentious issues are, first, whether there is a distinctively Marxian account of exploitation, second whether that account is without loss transposable into a discussion of justice in property rights,[1] and lastly whether a positive answer to the first question and a negative answer to the second mean that Marx is not so much saved as abandoned when he is defended by writers committed to 'methodological individualism'.[2] My answer to this last question is that he is; whether he ought to be abandoned is another question. I incline to think he ought, though I am conscious that this involves losses which are difficult to describe exactly, but which seem to me important.[3]

Let me begin by sketching a view of exploitation which *is* based on methodological individualism and the view of 'rational man' which classical economics up to and including Marshall would have accepted, and a view of justice which is (I think) that of untutored common sense. This is only a sketch, because its purpose is to illuminate Marx's enterprise by way of deepening the contrast between Marx and his individualist peers, and also because I shall come back to it in due course.

The minimum assumption behind rational man theories is that human behaviour is to be understood as the direction of effort to the attaining of goals by (what are reasonably believed to be) the best available means.[4] Of course, people very often do not employ the actually best available means, but in many areas their actions can be understood only if we suppose that they *think* the means they are employing are the best available. Where we think that what they have

---

[1] Roemer (1982).   [2] E.g., Elster (1985), pp. 5–8.   [3] Cf. Ryan (1987), pp. 130ff.
[4] Elster (1985), pp. 8–10.

29

done is a 'mistake', an explanation of their behaviour requires us to explain how they came to think that what were in fact bad means were good means. This requires us to separate out means and ends, and to treat 'rationality' in this context as a matter of the calculation of 'best means'. This account allows us to concede the claim that in practice actors usually 'satisfice' rather than 'optimise', though only if we can show that settling for 'good enough' is itself an optimising strategy.[5] What else the view will swallow is debatable; in Graham Allison's analysis of the Cuban Missile Crisis, the view that the Soviet government was a unitary rational actor is contrasted with the alternative analytical possibilities of treating its actions as the outcome of its military employing 'Standard Operating Procedures' for the installation of missiles and treating its actions as the by-product of political infighting.[6] But, this last is obviously consistent with treating the behaviour of Soviet political leaders as the actions of rational men and the behaviour of the Soviet government as the aggregate of those individual pieces of rational action; and Standard Operating Procedures may be understood as a rational solution to the problems of bureaucratic control and individual adherence to them be understood as the rational response of individuals to their bureaucratic environment. Indeed, it is hard to see what could persuade us that rational man analysis had *no* place in a social scientific explanation of any phenomenon, though it is much less hard to see what could persuade us not to treat complex organisations as if *they* were single, rational actors.

It is not surprising that little progress has been made since Weber in further refining the story – for, following Weber, we can say that *some* actions are to be understood as having an 'expressive' rationality, in the sense that it is doing them in that way which constitutes the goal, while others, and particularly those which students of economics are concerned with, are *Zweckrational*, i.e. display means–end rationality only.[7] This distinction agreed, we can tell a plausible story about the applicability of rational man theory to economics; the economy – the modern, competitive market economy – makes it extremely costly to hold false beliefs, and extremely costly to engage in purely expressive behaviour, though, of course, it may also be very costly to spend too much time in the pursuit of certainty, and industrial relations will be smoother if management engages in some behaviour expressive of a

---

[5] Hollis (1987), pp. 112ff.   [6] Allison (1971), pp. 82ff.
[7] Runciman (1978), pp. 28–30.

regard for the workforce as well as the profits. Rational man analysis falls naturally into two branches; first, there is what one ought to call 'normative' analysis. This is the calculation *a priori* of the action which agents with defined goals and adequate knowledge ought to take. A plausible analogy is offered by the analysis of moves in chess, where the analyst searches for the 'right' move – whether or not any player has played it.[8] Second, there is the explanation of what such agents actually get up to, where we have to insert the complicating factors of ignorance and the rest. At the explanatory level, we may make all kinds of adjustment to our focus – we may treat the actor as rational and well-informed and change our view of his goals, or we may treat his goals as obvious and see whether he was misinformed and why. The normative aspect of the enquiry takes logical priority; it is only if we know what the agent *ought* (rationally, of course, not morally) to have done that we know what requires explanation. Economics in the first sense is not an empirical discipline, any more than pure geometry, which equally lays down what *counts* as, say, an equilateral triangle, whether or not anyone has ever drawn one wholly accurately; economics in the second sense is. There is no great peculiarity about all this – subjects like population genetics which construct optimising models of how genes would act in order to promote their survival show considerable similarities.

To get from orthodox rational man to a theory of exploitation requires two steps. We first envisage rational men endowed with property rights in a variety of 'goods' – a term I use, *faute de mieux*, to cover anything which other people may want over which they have the rights of use and disposal at will, including therefore such things as their abilities, and their physical assets such as their beauty, along with external things. Standardly, rational man will engage in exchange with others in order to arrive at a set of holdings which he values more highly than the one he began with; entrepreneurial rational man will notice that putting bundles of goods together in various ways previously unnoticed by others yields a greater total utility, and he will accordingly make all sorts of intermediate deals with other people for the purchase or temporary use of their goods, taking to himself whatever portion of the added utility he can lawfully get. I need hardly emphasise that this is a highly idealised scheme; but it is one which captures much of the flavour of classical economic

[8] Hollis (1987), pp. 25–6.

thinking. It is worth noticing in passing that, although it explains entrepreneurial rewards in terms of the entrepreneur's claims on added utility, it does not make entrepreneurship into a factor of production – it is not an input whose productivity it makes sense to estimate.

We have supposed that people have property rights in their abilities and anything else of conceivable value; we must now suppose that we possess a sense of justice, according to which some bargains are 'unjust' or 'unfair' or excessively 'hard' bargains. For instance, it is perfectly possible – it used to happen – for a poor man to have to sell himself into slavery to obtain food, without there being any incoherence in the system of property rights under which the sale took place. So long as he can sell a freehold interest in himself, and so long as there are clear conventions for effecting the sale, there is no intellectual or conceptual difficulty in the transaction;[9] still, we may say that the man who will not let the poor man work and live on less onerous terms has driven an excessively hard bargain, and commits an injustice. In less strenuous examples, the same thing may be visible. The man who rents a piece of ground containing a gold seam may be able to employ others at wages which leave them slightly better off than starvation level, and take off an enormous income; that we may count as exploitation.[10] He has, we may say, no need to pay them as badly as that; he could have enough for himself and pay them a good deal more. We may go on to contrast his getting a huge return for merely happening to own the mine with their getting next to nothing for putting in all the dirty and dangerous effort required to get the gold.[11] In short, we look at who gets what share of the gains from cooperation, we apply notions of desert, thinking that effort and sacrifice deserve something, while mere luck does not.[12] We have a notion of people getting back a proper return for what they put in – more effort, more pay, less effort, less pay.[13] This is not our only thought, though some simple accounts suggest it is; we also tend to think that if something belongs to a man, others ought to have to pay for its use. Even if it costs me no effort to go and sing Rodolfo in *La Bohème*, it doesn't follow that other people are entitled to have me come sing for them for the asking; it's my voice and if I don't choose to use it, they must put up with it or offer me an inducement to do as

---

[9] Marx (1973), p. 501.   [10] Though not according to Nozick (1974), pp. 224–5.
[11] Rawls (1972), pp. 310–14.   [12] Sher (1987), pp. 97–108.   [13] Sher (1987).

they wish. But here, too, that thought is constrained by another, that I ought not to be unduly grasping about that inducement.

I put it all as simply as this for a purpose; rational man theories have to call in a theory of justice to decide when rational man's treatment of his fellows is 'exploitative'. It is not a simple matter to construct any such theory – as I hope to show at the end of this essay. But it is a simple matter to show that there are numerous intuitive notions about justice and ownership which we bring to bear on arguments about exploitation. Even a writer as hostile to the concept of exploitation as Robert Nozick can only sustain the affectation of not understanding what the expression means by reducing all rights to 'entitlements'; the ordinary man would, I suspect, think that a person could properly be said to be standing on his entitlements but to be exploiting others while he was doing so.[14] An inventor who set a price on a new drug which only the very rich could afford would commonly be said to be exploiting the sickness of others, even if people found it hard to decide whether he was, as the owner of the stuff, *entitled* to sell it to whomever he wanted at whatever price they would pay, or, in virtue of his exploitative behaviour, no longer entitled to it at all. A century and a quarter ago, John Stuart Mill observed that in such cases we waver between saying that a person ought not to do what he is entitled to and denying that he is entitled to do it at all.[15] A fully paid up theory of exploitation would have to be a theory about the basis of ownership and the admissibility of transactions of various different classes.[16]

Marx does not approach the issue in this way at all. He knew of the Ricardian socialists, and their view that the individual's right to his own labour entailed that capitalists must be robbing their workers; and he knew of Proudhon's view that it was the absence of free credit which allowed exploitative property owning to persist.[17] His own account of exploitation was not to rest on any such fragile foundation as a theory of natural right; the account of exploitation he offered was to be a contribution to 'science' not a moral critique of capitalist relations. Marx's view of morality is itself a large subject,[18] but in outline the bearing of it on our topic is this. There is no such thing as a realm of values, the realm of the 'ought' as opposed to the 'is'; it is not that moral ideas have *no* impact on what happens in society, but the

---

[14] Nozick (1974), pp. 181–2.   [15] Ryan (ed.) (1987a), p. 337.
[16] Nozick (1974), pp. 170ff.   [17] Marx (n.d.), p. 225.   [18] But see Lukes (1986).

way they have an effect is, as with all ideas, by way of their impact on people's behaviour. If I think that cyanide is almond essence and flavour my food with it, I shall die; a 'falsehood' has caused my death, not because there are such things as falsehoods operating on our lives, but because the explanation of my death has to invoke my false belief. Marx's insistence that there are no moral ideals operating in an ideal realm relies on such a perspective; it looks uninteresting to us, but was more interesting in his own day, since he had grown up with Young Hegelians who really did seem to believe in the causal effectiveness of Equality or Justice or Liberty.[19] More importantly, Marx would not appeal to the *morality* of socialism both because he thought that most people would adjust their moral responses to their interests, and because he thought that justice as generally understood would seem to most observers to be on the side of capitalism.[20]

Marx's account of these things is one of the most interesting peripheral elements in his work. Since he saw societies as essentially productive engines, fated to operate whatever distributive principles enabled them to employ the productive forces at their disposal, he inevitably thought that both property rights and the conceptions of justice which legitimated them were determined by the mode of production at issue. Ancient societies employed slaves, were committed to property in people, and in some sense had to have a theory of justice such as Aristotle's which held that what was just was what was suitable to people of different sorts, and slaves were people of a different sort from their owners, justly owned by them, and justly, therefore, handing over to them everything they produced. In such a society, the individual who set out to make larger profits than was proper to his station was neither rational nor irrational, but a menace to polite society. His behaviour was 'unnatural', and he showed a lack of the moderation which men ought to display in all social dealings. That this ethic was important Marx never doubted; in the *Grundrisse*, he appeals to it in partial explanation of the non-development of capitalism in ancient Greece.[21] Still, the crucial thing is the implications of this approach for Marx's understanding of justice within capitalism. Capitalism could only survive if legitimated by an appropriate conception of justice; this had to be adapted to the marketplace and congruent with people's expectations of the market-

---

[19] Marx and Engels (1965), pp. 29–30.
[20] Indeed, Wood (1972) argues that according to Marx capitalism *is* just.
[21] Marx (1973), pp. 787–8.

place. It therefore had to be a conception of justice as justice in exchange, based on the principle that equals had to exchange for equals; unequal exchanges were presumptively unjust. Moreover, since people are not entirely unaware of what is going on around them, much of the working of capitalism had actually to obey that principle – visible robbery, in the form of employers ratting on their contracts of employment and the like would have created chaos; and, indeed, every employer other than the defaulter had a real interest in the maintenance of a system which would enforce justice at this level against employers tempted to default.[22]

This bears on the theory of exploitation in the following way. Marx needed, as a matter of theoretical urgency, to give an account of the generation of profit; this account had to be couched within the framework of the labour theory of value; it also had, as a political matter, to represent profit as taken from the worker, but without any suggestion that fair wages could replace present taking. The problem Marx faced is well known; if all commodities exchanged at their true values, profit was deeply mysterious; how could assembling the commodities bought at t_1 make them worth more at t_2. Marx was, for deep and somewhat inscrutable reasons, convinced that profit was created in production and only realised in exchange and therefore *had* to explain the appearance and appropriation of the surplus in the process of production itself. In Marx the primacy of production over exchange is an obsession, but he is right to distinguish the capitalist manufacturer's profit from the merchant's profit, only wrong to overlook the fact that there are accounts of entrepreneurship which satisfy this thought, in a non-Marxian way. If he could show profit being created at the very moment of creation, he could also show that demands for 'fair wages' were nonsense. It was futile to try to tinker with the distributive aspect of the economy only, as the *Critique of the Gotha Programme* argues repeatedly.[23]

The explanation of how the capitalist bought all his inputs at their full value, sold his output at no more than its full value, and managed to make a profit in the process is the best known part of Marx's economic theory. One of the capitalist's inputs was 'labour power', the worker's capacity to labour for his employer; the exchange value of this was, like the exchange value of anything else, equal to its cost of production, in other words, equal to the cost of the consumption

[22] Marx (1976), I, p. 280.   [23] Marx and Engels (n.d.), II, p. 25.

goods which enabled the worker to appear and be ready for work. This subsistence wage was what workers tended to be paid; they therefore got the full value of their labour power at the point where any visible exchange took place. The capitalist could properly say that he paid as much as he could afford, since if he paid more than the going rate, he'd go broke; if he paid less, his workers would move to other employers. On average, therefore, workers must be paid the full value of their labour power. But labour power is peculiar among commodities in that when it is used up it adds more to the commodities on which it is used than went into its original creation. Machinery and raw materials only add as much exchange value as they contain; since they embody dead or frozen labour, they are incapable of generating additional value. Alone among commodities, labour power has the peculiarity that when it is used – i.e. turned into actual labouring – it adds more exchange value than it cost. The capitalist thus buys labour power at its value, and gets the value added by the workers in the course of production. Capitalist exploitation consists, as does all exploitation, in the expropriator of surplus value getting something for which he has not paid. But, unlike earlier forms of exploitation where the unpaid labour of the worker was visible in the form of slavery or the labour services of medieval peasants and the like, unpaid labour under capitalism is hidden in the heart of the production process, disguised by the form of the wage bargain, and therefore in need of revelation by Marx's analytical techniques.[24]

This relates to Marx's view of justice in an obvious way. Marx, who always held that capitalism embodied 'contradictions' of various kinds, was enabled by this argument to claim that capitalism both did (on the surface) and did not (in reality) live up to its own standard of justice. It is not that Marx invokes in his own person the standards of capitalism *in order to* criticise capitalism in their light – Marx is really not very interested in those standards, as standards – nor yet that he criticises capitalism by the standards of socialism – as we shall soon see, it is quite hard to say what those standards are, and a waste of time to quarrel about the sense in which they are 'moral' standards. What Marx does is employ capitalism's own standard of justice in an essentially *ad hominem* fashion; it is not he, but the defenders of capitalism who should be embarrassed by the failure of capitalism to

[24] Marx (1976), I, pp. 279–80.

live up to the standard of justice which it is forced to preach and by its very nature forced also to violate.[25]

Those who are exploited are forced by their lack of resources to part with the surplus value which is thus extracted from them. This part of Marx's account is, of course, the part which is most readily translated into the language of individualist, rational man theories of exploitation; the capitalists' possession of the capital funds required for production allows them to sit out any resistance to subsistence wages which the workers may try to put up, and, in classic, Mill-like fashion, their taking off the entire surplus can be explained in terms of the inelastic demand for employment on the side of the workers, who must have employment or starve. Why is this not all that Marx is saying; why should I insist that Marx's holism demands that we should read its implications in a way no individualist would accept?

On my view of it, Marx was interested in the specifically capitalist form of property relations which underpin this process and not so much in the universal fact of unequal bargaining strength leading to exploitative bargains. He always objected to what he thought of as the truistic universal formulations of Mill and others like him, for what he was impressed by was the fact that under capitalism the surplus appears only in the form of surplus *value*, and the unpaid labour of the worker is not apparent in the way it is under slavery and serfdom. It is the abstract quality of the relationship which makes it peculiar to capitalism. To see the process as the individualists see it is to give too many hostages to fortune; it suggests that, since exploitation occurs because of an unjust system of property rights, the cure must be to set up a just system of property rights. This was Mill's solution, and it leads naturally to his defence of producer cooperatives and market socialism (of a very under-described kind).[26] Marx's sights were set altogether higher. What dominates his thinking is the thought that property as such dominates the entire social order of capitalism; capital's relationship to the workers' efforts is characterised in religious and demonological metaphors, which have a tremendous metaphysical loading. *Le Mort saisit le Vif* is Marx's constant cry; dead labour battens on live labour, the vampire seeks an unholy existence on the blood of the living. This is not mere rhetoric, but the key to Marx's vision, and a reflection in evaluation of the fact that he does not build his explanation of

---

[25] Geras (1986), pp. 16–18, argues energetically against this view.
[26] Mill (1968), V, pp. 703ff.

macroscopic economic relationships on the strategic interaction of individuals, but the reverse. It is not the creation of just property institutions that he is after, but the abolition of anything we could properly describe as property or ownership; all such institutions allow the reign of dead things over living men.

None the less, in visualising the abolition of property and the ending of exploitation, Marx moves in two steps, as *The Critique of the Gotha Programme* suggests. Under stage one of socialism, capitalist conceptions of rights and capitalist notions of justice will continue to impress people; with the capitalists gone, there will be no class of exploiters who cream off the surplus and dispose of it according to their own wishes, but there will still be a need to reward people differently according to their contributions to society. Although no parasitical group now takes a part of the surplus created by the efforts of the workers, there is never the less no question of giving the workers the full value of their work, if by that we mean that they will receive it in their wage packet – hence all Marx's ferocious attacks on the demand that workers should get the full value of their labour, a demand which, we can now see, is either met already under capitalism, or is one which cannot – in that shape – be met under socialism or any other social system.[27] But, over a lifetime the workers will, on average, get a full return for what they contribute; the 'deductions' from current value which are needed for educating the young, providing pensions for the old, paying for research and development, and all the rest of the investment bill, will come back to them one way and another, since nobody else is taking any of the value they create merely because of happening to own the capital employed in the industries they work in. (Those who die young will get more than they contribute, those who die immediately after ceasing work will get less, those who live to a great age will get more; all that is on offer is justice for the average worker.) In effect, socialism of the lower stage as Marx envisages it can achieve what capitalism has to promise, namely equal rewards for equal contributions.

But this is only a transitional stage. After that stage, the narrow horizons of bourgeois right are transcended, we expect each to contribute according to ability and each to receive according to need – 'need' being understood, not in the sense of bare necessities, but in

---

[27] *Marx Engels Selected Works*, II, p. 22.

Marx's phrase as the needs of humanly developed man. This is not a principle of distributive justice;[28] rights have vanished from the moral lexicon; indeed, morality has vanished from the lexicon too.[29] It is a practical, not a moral, principle; that is, we all understand why we live according to the principle, we understand that it is a matter of our choice, and we understand that our choice is not arbitrary. 'Moral' principles in Marx's dismissive account are such because they are misunderstood; we think of them as categorical imperatives, the dictates of reason, the Voice of God or whatever, and we cannot see them as rules of practice just like the rules of practice which guide the rest of our behaviour. But this mystification is itself only a facet of what the pre-human world does to keep itself going; it survives by bewildering its victims. Once out of its clutches, we can see our rules of practice for what they are; because there will be no conflicts of interest, there will be no need for bamboozlement, and it will drop away.

In all this, the rational individual of non-Marxist theory scarcely gets a look in. Contrary to Cohen, who tries to get us to accept his account of Marx's 'functional' theory by appealing to our existing belief in rational man, the creature who tries to achieve his goals as efficiently as possible and therefore puts pressure on the productive forces, Marx himself insists that the 'rational man' of orthodox economic theory is a social creation and one which is in fact both recent and local.[30] Nor, of course, does Marx think that the participants in a capitalist economy are rational in any stronger sense than that. Marx insists that behaviour which outsiders might think 'irrational' is to be understood only as behaviour which the going economic and social system forces upon the participants in that system. It is not 'rational' *tout court* to prefer making money to gratifying our sense of honour, but we may safely bet that, under capitalism, the managing director of a large manufacturing concern will sacrifice honour to money where that is necessary. (I do not mean to endorse everything Marx says about this; I incline to think that Veblen was right to call attention to the similarities between the conspicuous consumption of captains of industry and clan chieftains, and I have no great faith in the accuracy of the motivational assumptions of orthodox economic theory.) Again it may by most standards not be rational for a man to make the sacrifices necessary

[28] See Geras (1986), pp. 47ff, for the opposite view.   [29] Ryan (1987b).
[30] Marx (1973), pp. 100ff.

for success as a capitalist; we may deplore the damage he does to his relationships with family and friends, and to his own emotional life – but that is neither here nor there for Marx's *explanatory* purposes; all that matters is that enough people are socialised into the beliefs and aims which keep the system operating in a self-perpetuating manner. Cohen's account, which makes it a fact of human nature that mankind is rational in the orthodox sense, makes it surprising that capitalism failed to develop much earlier than it did in fact; Marx's explanation of pre-capitalist economic formations may not amount to anything very striking – it tells us next to nothing about why non-traditional and calculating modes of thought triumphed over their rivals in modern Europe and nowhere else – but it does not obliterate the problem by supposing that people have always and everywhere been rational calculators.[31] The point makes a considerable difference to much else in Marx. Peter Singer's account of Marx, for instance, explains Marx's hostility to capitalism in terms of capitalism's inefficiency at reconciling individual and social costs and benefits, so that the characteristic defect of capitalism would be exemplified in the miserable state of public transport.[32] But, this pitches the point too low. One could envisage all sorts of tinkering with pricing policies and the like which would cope with Singer's criticisms; Marx's attack on capitalist irrationality rests on the difference between our having the preferences we do because they have been foisted upon us by the system and our having them because they are 'human'. It is not only a matter of criticising the capitalist system as 'individually rational and socially irrational', as the radical but orthodox might. Marx wants to throw out this way of conceiving matters along with the economic order which makes them appropriate. It may be true at the level of empirical, unanalysed description that men and women in capitalist society behave like rational men in the classical economist's story; but that is their misfortune.

Now, if this is plausible, what I've so far claimed is that the account of exploitation within capitalism which Marx offers is distinctively Marxian and unorthodox, because it cannot be detached from the theory of value – because what is peculiar to capitalism is that capital sucks surplus value from living labour; more importantly, I have shown that the order of causal priority in Marx's account is the reverse of that in any account which explains exploitation as the

<hr />

[31] G.A. Cohen (1978), pp. 152ff.   [32] Singer (1982).

result of rational individuals employing their property in such a way that the non-owners of property end up consistently on the wrong side of all the bargains. Marx's account is holistic and systemic, in that it is the demand of capital for further value which accounts for individual behaviour, both in the sense of structuring motivation and structuring the situation which individuals face. It seems to me a point in favour of this view of what Marx was up to that it gets round a familiar problem, that of why individuals unite into classes. Cohen's account of Marx has been objected to as omitting Marx's own stress on class conflict;[33] it is an explicable omission, since in his version of Marx the causal mechanism invoked is an individualist one, into which classes fit at best rather awkwardly. To remedy the omission of classes and class-conflict within this framework, we have to explain the way individuals unite into classes as the collective consequence of each individual's purchase of an insurance policy, much in the way we explain individuals uniting into one people under a sovereign in Hobbes's *Leviathan*. And, as all discussions of the Prisoners' Dilemma have observed, there is no way we can generate the appropriate story from the egoistic premises such theories begin with. Marx may properly be criticised for over-confidence in his own assumption that societies simply do structure themselves around exploitative relationships, but it is clearly his confidence that the system as a totality would generate 'appropriate' allegiances that makes him suppose that classes and class loyalty would be one element so created. It is not my aim to show that Marx's confident functionalism was right – only that it was essential.[34]

My account is not novel. Indeed, it is in the same tradition as Sorel's view that one of the virtues of Marxism was that it represented workers and capitalists alike as doomed by their fate to fight the battles of the capitalist economy.[35] The Greeks and Trojans, playthings of the Gods, never saw their battles as something to blame one another for in the fashion of individualistic, bourgeois morality; no more ought the proletarians to blame the capitalists for their harsh behaviour; when they waged the class war the proletarians should do so without rancour or individual hatred. Capitalists are the slaves of their capital, forced to fight for their vampire master. The workers are forced to fight back. The only 'virtues' to be esteemed in these conditions are classical ones, such as fortitude and initiative in

---

[33] J. Cohen (1980), reviewing G.A. Cohen (1978).
[34] Cf. Elster (1985), pp. 29–37.   [35] Sorel (1961).

battle. Moralising is no use to anyone; firstly, nobody takes any notice, and secondly, it produces terrible recriminations and cruelty if things go wrong.[36]

The mere fact that this account is not novel is no recommendation if it leaves Marx in a wholly incoherent posture. One claim that it does might be mounted along the lines adopted by Jon Elster. Elster argues that methodological individualism is inescapable, and, of course, if it is, then holistic Marxism only contains as much truth as is translatable into individualistic terms.[37] My reply is that it is not methodological individualism that is inescapable (where this involves the assumption of orthodox rational man and the view that the order of causal priority runs from the individual to the system). What is inescapable is what one might call 'methodological particularism', that is, the insistence that, for any given instantiation of a system, there has to be a particular causal route for the production of the system's effects. The way in which a heat-seeking missile, or one of Grey Walter's mechanical tortoises or a horse finding its way back to the stable achieve their 'homewards' paths is specific to each of them; they are all of them home-finding systems none the less. The supposed attractions of methodological individualism are really the attractions of the truism that no system can work, except in some particular way or other; when asked how it works, the proper reply is to produce its wiring diagram, or in the case of a social system the motivational and intellectual equipment of the individuals whose behaviour, appropriately aggregated, is that of the system. But, to be a holist is not to deny any of that. Rather, it's to bet on the prospect of explaining social and economic phenomena by approaching them in a 'system-down' rather than an 'individuals-up' perspective – just as we might think that in order to understand the internal structure of the heat-seeking missile, say, we had to start with its working at the level of a whole self-regulating system. Whether social systems are best approached in this fashion is an empirical, not a philosophical or methodological issue.[38] In that sense, Althusser's demand for a structuralist Marxism was true to the spirit of Marx's enterprise; but his Spinozistic theory of knowledge was not. On Marx's account of it, just as different 'home-seeking' devices would produce the same effects by different means, so different capitalist economies would produce the same effects, often by different means; they would create the institutions

---

[36] Sorel (1961).   [37] Elster (1985), pp. 5–8.   [38] Miller (1984), pp. 221–36.

and individuals complete with their attitudes and beliefs which would sustain the (internally contradictory as well as integrated) system. If the Marxian research programme had worked, this guiding image would have produced an economics and a history and a sociology of a distinctive kind.[39]

I say 'if the programme had worked'; I do not mean that it has been a wholesale failure, but I cannot believe that it has been a thoroughgoing success. All too often, the best work in a Marxian framework has been indistinguishable from the best work done merely eclectically. But, my aim is not to press that point, so much as to insist that there is a genuine parting of the ways between non-truistic methodological individualism – that is, the research programme based on orthodox rational man analysis – and Marxism. To adopt an individualist perspective is to admit that the Marxian research programme has not worked. Bits and pieces of it can still be pillaged, of course; but those who pillage bits and pieces call themselves 'Marxists' mostly out of a sort of nostalgia for the political allegiances of their youth.[40] There is, of course, nothing wrong with intellectual grave robbery; one may decently borrow whatever helps one to think about difficult topics. None the less, rather than trying to patch together the theory which Marx might have come up with if he had been brought up on the theory of games rather than on Hegel and Savigny, perhaps we ought to grit our teeth and decide either that the attractions of Marx's picture are such that we should ignore the signs of 'degeneration' in the research programme, such as the interminable quibbles over the definition of 'class', 'state', 'mode of production', or that we must live without the pleasures of Marx's dramatic picture of our condition and learn to make the most of a more piecemeal approach. If we settle for this second view, the property-rights based approach to exploitation seems the most plausible approach; and anyone who hankers after a tradition to belong to may be comforted by the thought that behind Mill and Smith lie Locke, Suarez, Aquinas, Aristotle and Plato. But, as the length of that list suggests, what we are likely to find is that 'exploitation' will be no more than one small aspect of the whole topic of social and economic justice.

---

[39] Elster (1985), pp. 29ff.
[40] This renders a bit brusquely the upshot of the introductory remarks in G.A. Cohen (1989) and Elster (1985), p. 531.

A theory of exploitation is an account of how people employ their ownership of the means of production to grab more of the results of productive cooperation than they are entitled to (according to some, yet to be developed, theory of justice). Those who are exploited are all those who fail to get what they might, because their lack of property prevents them from forcing others to concede it. Anyone who makes a genuinely free gift to someone else is not exploited, so the fact that the exploited are forced to accept less than they are entitled to must be part of the definition of exploitation. Now, the following difficulty seems to loom. Suppose we think, as we might, that an obvious starting point for cooperation is for everyone to have an equally acceptable set of property rights – defined either objectively, or via a Walrasian or Dworkinian auction – and for titles to follow uncoerced contracts. This seems to ensure that every bargain will have been acceptable to the contracting parties, and we must hope that we have defined property rights in the first place in such a way that they take care of third parties whose position is worsened by contracts to which they are not parties. (I sell software in competition with two other people; if they combine forces and benefit from their pooled talents, my competitive position is weakened; does a theory of initial equality have to have an answer to the question whether I can ask for compensation from them?) Still, there will be a crux; these bargains will distribute the results in a way the initial auction would not have done if the goods resulting from the bargains had been 'manna from heaven'. Does this mean they are exploitative?

So far as I can see, there are three avenues down which we may go. The first is to insist that anything other than equal shares of all the benefits of cooperation must be exploitative; any differential distribution represents something like an illicit rental taken off because of a strong bargaining position. The fact that others are prepared to pay a high price for the added benefits they get – Beatles tickets could go to £50 and find willing buyers – makes no difference to the moral position. This view seems to me to be consistent enough in itself; it is unMarxist in making equality a fundamental value, and in accepting a half-way house on the route to abolishing property rights altogether, but that is no objection. That it conflicts with other values may be more of a problem. It may be that the price of equality is that entrepreneurs do not come forward to innovate, and that the entire economy operates at a lower level than it might, and that everyone is therefore much worse off than anyone would be under a less egalitarian system, and we have sacrificed welfare to equality. It may even be argued that a new form of exploitation has replaced the one we have abolished – the least able have deprived the more able of what they might blamelessly have had, because the least able can insist on nobody being better off than they. Rawls, of course, rests his whole theory on the first point, and therefore offers a theory of justice which is what we might call a modified egalitarian theory.[41] Dworkin's reflections on equality are in much the same spirit.[42] It is easy to see the force of such modifications of egalitarianism; what, after all, is the point of not being 'exploited' if we are materially worse off as a result? In Marx's account, which tied exploitation to a real-life economy in which workers' wages are constantly driven down to subsistence level, the abolition of exploitation goes hand in hand with an increase in the welfare of the worker. What if it doesn't, as in this sort of picture? Purists will observe that in a Rawlsian perspective, 'exploitation' loses its connection with the ownership of capital or the means of life generally, but that Rawls's theory does abolish exploitation in two familiar senses, first in preventing the better endowed from driving too hard a bargain for the use of their endowments, second in securing that the less endowed are not taken advantage of and driven to accept excessively hard bargains.

Pure egalitarianism, and to a lesser extent Rawls's theory, too, runs into conflicts with our attachment to voluntarism. So important is voluntarism as a component of theories of justice that many writers, of whom Nozick is perhaps the best known current representative, would rely on the principle of *volenti non fit injuria* to claim that it is the voluntariness of agreements that rules out exploitation. This, the second of the three approaches I have in mind, is sceptical of Marx's view that the exploited get less than the value of their contributions, because it doubts the possibility of assessing the value of the contributions of the people who supply the inputs. We cannot achieve a situation in which each is requited exactly for what he or she contributes (and even if we could, there'd be much to be said against disturbing voluntarily made agreements to achieve it); egalitarian theories deal with the problem of our inability to give an objective assessment of the value of inputs by saying that, whoever produces the final output, everyone gets an equal or a 'minimax'-based claim on it. Nozick deals with it by dropping any attempt to ask what the

[41] Rawls (1972), pp. 100ff.   [42] Dworkin (1981).

value of efforts is to other people, or what the share of value is that each person contributes; everyone gets whatever anyone else is willing to exchange for what's offered, and so long as nobody inhibits anyone in seeking the best bargain they can, there is no exploitation. Capitalist entrepreneurs do not get paid for adding value; they simply have a title to whatever it is they've bargained for. Nozick agrees that pure or modified egalitarianism of the sort discussed above is a possibility, but an intolerable one, and opts instead for voluntarism. The difficulty which voluntarism faces in its turn is that it has to offer an account of the justices of the initial entitlements from which the process of voluntary exchange begins. This is why Nozick is concerned with initial acquisition and why Marx devotes such energy to showing that the 'so-called primitive accumulation' amounted to the forced expropriation of small freeholders.[43] *If* capitalists had been able to tell the right story about the pedigree of their property rights, Marx would have been vastly more embarrassed than he was. As it was, he could point out that the system had begun in theft and carried on in the same vein. How relevant Nozick thinks his 'state of nature' theory of acquisition is to the justice or exploitativeness of present day economic arrangements is unclear. It looks very much as if he believes that existing holdings all too often originated in force and fraud, so that the abolition of exploitation, or the achievement of justice, requires a once for all redistribution along Rawlsian lines – after that, a utopian degree of justice can be achieved as all holdings will have arisen by legitimate transfers from a legitimate origin.[44]

A third view, which is a possible interpretation of Hayek's challenge to the idea of social justice, is that the concept of exploitation ought to be abandoned, because everything distinctive in the concept of exploitation is suspect, and everything not suspect can be dealt with by arguments about justice in its acceptable form, or arguments about coercion. We might differ from Nozick by thinking that there was no hope of finding a pedigree for most holdings, and argue that 'exploitation' is to be expelled from the moral lexicon except as a term for forced (i.e. contra-legally forced) takings from recognised property holders. Even in this framework, it is recognised that, even if the least favoured are not *exploited*, they do pose a moral problem. We ought to be able to explain why they do worse than

---

[43] Marx (1976), I, pp. 873ff.   [44] Nozick (1974), pp. 230–1.

other people, even if we cannot explain in any very persuasive way that they *deserve* no more or are *morally* (as opposed to legally) entitled to no more. Curiously, Hayek's answer is like Rawls's – we can say to the worst off person in the capitalist order that he or she is better off than the worst favoured would be under any other economic order. That he or she is the worst off person is no doubt bad luck – but all it is is bad *luck*; it is not exploitation so long as his or her legally recognised property rights are not infringed. This needs, and Hayek provides, an account of what property rights the law should create, and of what constraints there must be on how these can be altered by legislative or judicial changes. All this is persuasively done by Hayek; but there remains a tension which he cannot quite defuse. The proposition that all is well because what people get is a matter of luck, and the worst off do better than the worst off anywhere else do is only acceptable if it is incontestable that 'luck' determines all the outcomes. The worst off person might be forgiven for thinking that how well people are going to do is more predictable than the 'luck' theory would suggest. Moreover, even if the worst off person under a different system of entitlements would be worse off than the currently worst off person, the currently worst off may plausibly claim that he or she is badly off as a result of exploitation, while still agreeing that this exploitation increased GNP in the aggregate, and acknowledging that the distributive mechanism made the worst off better off than other 'worst-offs'. The notion underlying the complaint of exploitation in a 'property-rights' perspective is just that other people were unfairly able to throw their economic weight about, in a way which he or she could not resist.[45]

This is, of course, all very sketchy and incomplete. I mean it only to show something familiar from other contexts: when we try to tackle questions about justice and exploitation along these lines, we almost at once run into tensions between aggregative and distributive concerns, between historical and forward looking concerns and between principles which concentrate on the fate of identifiable individuals and those which concentrate on classes of persons. This would not constitute an objection to this way of discussing the issue of exploitation for anyone who accepted the need for a piecemeal explanation of economic relations and a piecemeal assessment of

[45] Hayek (1973–9).

their justice and injustice, but it provides a last confirmation of my earlier claim that this isn't the way Marx tackled the issue. For the great attraction of his holistic, systemic, amoral account of exploitation is precisely that everything seems to hang together – explanation, criticism and prediction at once. If we have to put up with something less compelling, we ought not to blink the fact that it is less compelling.

References

Allison, G.T. (1971), *Essence of Decision*, Boston: Little Brown.

Cohen, G.A. (1978), *Karl Marx's Theory of History: A Defence*, Oxford: Clarendon Press.

(1989), *History, Freedom and Justice*, Oxford: Clarendon Press.

Cohen, J. (1980), Review of Cohen (1978), *Journal of Philosophy*, 79: 253–73.

Dworkin, R. (1981), 'What is Equality?', *Philosophy and Public Affairs*, 10: 185–246, 283–345.

Elster, J. (1985), *Making Sense of Marx*, Cambridge University Press.

Geras, N. (1986), 'The Controversy about Marx and Justice', *Literature of Revolution*, London: Verso.

Hayek, F.A. (1973–9), *Law, Liberty and Legislation*, 3 vols., London: Routledge Kegan Paul.

Hollis, M. (1987), *The Cunning of Reason*, Cambridge University Press.

Lukes, S. (1986), *Marxism and Morality*, Oxford University Press.

Marx, K. (1973), *Grundrisse*, Harmondsworth: Penguin Books.

(1976), *Capital*, Harmondsworth: Penguin Books.

(n.d.), *The Poverty of Philosophy*, Moscow: Foreign Languages Publishing House.

Marx, K. and Engels, F. (1965), *The German Ideology*, London: Lawrence and Wishart.

(n.d.), *Marx Engels Selected Works*, Moscow: Foreign Languages Publishing House.

Mill, J.S. (1968), 'Chapters on Socialism', *Collected Works*, Toronto: Toronto University.

Miller, R.W. (1984), *Analyzing Marx*, Princeton: Princeton University Press.

Nozick, R. (1974), *Anarchy, State and Utopia*, Oxford: Basil Blackwell.

Rawls, J. (1972), *A Theory of Justice*, Oxford: Clarendon Press.

Roemer, J. (1982), 'Property Relations vs. Surplus Value in Marxian Exploitation', *Philosophy and Public Affairs*, 11: 281–313.

Runciman, W.G. (ed.) (1978), *Weber: Selections in Translation*, Cambridge University Press.

Ryan, A. (ed.) (1987a), *Mill and Bentham: Utilitarianism and Other Essays*, Harmondsworth: Penguin Books.

(1987b), 'Justice, Exploitation and the End of Morality', in J.D.G. Evans (ed.), *Moral Philosophy and Contemporary Problems*, Cambridge University Press

Sher, G. (1987), *Desert*, Princeton: Princeton University Press.

Singer, P. (1982), *Marx*, Oxford University Press.

Sorel, G. (1961), *Reflections on Violence*, translated by Hulme, T.E. and Roth, J., London: Collier-Macmillan.

Wood, A. (1972), 'The Marxian Critique of Justice', *Philosophy and Public Affairs*, 1: 244–82.

5 Pleasures, prices and principles

TONY CRAMP

I

Introduction

It was a bold lecturer who began his course by saying, 'My topic is linear algebra. I believe that a lecturer should declare his position. I propose to teach linear algebra from a Christian point of view.' However, given that economics has more obvious ethical connotations than does mathematics, I may perhaps be judged less bold in proposing to assess critically the philosophical foundations of economics – and in particular its assumption of rational utility maximisation – from a position of explicit Christian allegiance.

The great charm of economic theory (Dennis Robertson once observed) is that, if you stand in one place long enough, discarded ideas come round again. This is certainly true of the utilitarian basis of market theory, as Joseph Schumpeter pointed out. Reflecting late nineteenth century disillusion with utilitarianism, he branded it 'the shallowest of all conceivable philosophies of life'; claimed that it was possible nevertheless to 'salvage much of economic analysis that at first sight seems hopelessly vitiated by utilitarian preconceptions'; but then was forced to recognise that the death-sentence on utilitarianism in economics was premature, for 'the corpse shows signs of life'.[1]

However, utilitarianism is a complex phenomenon. Is it mistaken then to refer to *the* utilitarian basis of market theory? I think not, but the point needs to be addressed. For there are three main varieties of utilitarian ethical injunction, differing principally with regard to the prescribed maximand:

(1) Bentham's hedonism (egoism) emphasising that the gap between the sum of pleasures and the sum of pains should be maximised;

---

[1] Schumpeter (1954), pp. 133, 134 and 1068.

(2) Moore's ideal utilitarianism, advocating the maximisation of 'good states of mind';
(3) Mill's so-called eudaimonistic (ethical) variety, with stress on satisfaction from such desiderata as justice in society.

When Mill argued[2] that utilitarianism is 'not only not a godless doctrine, but [is] more profoundly religious than any other', he doubtless had his own brand (3) in mind; I shall revert to it, and argue its lack of relation to orthodox economics. Moore's brand was clearly formulated too late to have been the historical basis for market theory, fully mature by the time of the marginal revolution of the 1870s. My case is that Benthamite hedonism is the variety of utilitarian reasoning which keeps on popping in and out of economic theory; and that this tergiversation is the inevitable outcome of its clear deficiencies, combined with the inability of secularist economic reasoning to discover a viable alternative.

Economics having (regrettably) attempted to cut loose from its earlier moorings in moral philosophy, it may be best to begin from more familiar territory than the foregoing. Private greed and private rationality (according to one eminent economist, proclaiming clearly in a perhaps unguarded moment ideas that are usually shrouded in technicalities) are the twin axioms of economic theory; I believe that he was right with regard to the spirit, if not always to the letter. This paper's basic argument on the critical side is that this claim:

(a) has Bentham-style utilitarian foundation or *no* foundation, for clear-sighted empirical observation (if indeed it is possible to escape from Kuhnian tunnel-vision to make such observation) cannot establish it and does not support it;
(b) cannot be understood save in historical perspective, as is indicated by Gunnar Myrdal's dictum[3] that

We must look upon the majority of modern economic doctrines as modified reminiscences of very old political thinking conceived in days when a teleological meaning and a normative purpose were more openly part of the subject matter of economics.

The next section of this paper will develop part (b) of this argument by critically examining in turn the historical development of the terms of the eminent economist's aphorism, as a preparation for the main critique of them in section III.

---

[2] Mill (1874), chapter 2, para. 21.   [3] Myrdal (1953), p. x.

II

Historical overview

First, why *axioms*? Because of the dominance in economics of the geometrical method of René Descartes (1596–1650),[4] which was to be taken over by Thomas Hobbes (1588–1679), Bentham's forerunner in developing a utilitarian basis for market theory.

Descartes's problem was that of doubt. Hitherto, knowledge had been regarded as descriptive of a reality accessible to the senses. Sense-impressions had suggested that the sun goes round a static earth. But if Copernicus and Galileo were right, the earth goes round the sun, and appearances can be false. How, then, to attain reliable knowledge? The answer lay in the use of the geometrical method, to whose development Descartes himself made such a distinguished contribution. In the manner of proofs of geometrical theorems, begin from axioms, indisputable truths. Proceed by logical steps, and you can arrive at incontrovertible, even though far from obvious, conclusions.

It was Hobbes, older than Descartes but longer-lived, who was the leader in applying Cartesian principles to human affairs. In implicit acceptance of what might now be called monistic methodological ideas, what was good for natural science could on his reasoning be expected to be fruitful in social science also. Reason was common to all men; its application on the basis of sound method must lead to agreement on human and social issues. It was an attractive programme. The trouble (as is obvious to us, but was shielded from Hobbes in his mono-cultural world) is that the 'axioms' of economic theory, far from being genuinely axiomatic, are open to fundamental challenge.

Second, why *private*? Because of the dominance in western culture of an atomistic, as opposed to a holistic, understanding of the life of society. Atomism is doubly influential, for it has come to characterise scientific method as well as prevailing social doctrine. Hobbes was again a pioneer in the latter field, but in the former the thought of Immanuel Kant (1724–1804) was influential.

Like Descartes, Kant was troubled by the problem of achieving

---

[4] Mini (1974), p. 15: 'From France, Cartesianism spread to England via the works of Locke and Hume. And through them it spread to economics, determining its nature and character down to our own days.'

reliable knowledge. His difficulties, however, were greater than the Frenchman's, because David Hume (1711–76) had convinced him that, in addition to the possible falsity of appearances, their empirical regularity could not be relied upon: we cannot *know* that the sun will rise tomorrow. Kant, who said that 'I woke from my slumbers when I read Hume', sought for progress amid possible chaos via his 'Copernican revolution' which proposed to supplant reason's old passive role, in which it was regarded as providing a copy of reality, by a new active role. The inner reality of things, after Hume, must indeed be recognised as inaccessible to human reason. The outer appearances or *phenomena*, however, could be reduced to order by breaking reality down into its simplest elements, and then reconstructing it by the power of ordering thought. Henceforth, order could no longer be assumed to reside in the reality under examination, but must be imposed upon it by the reasoning observer. Whatever may be the case for natural science, there is no blinking the significance of these ideas for social science, seeking to discover an order underlying apparently chaotic surface complexity. Order is in the mind of the observer, and if observers consistently disagree, the prospect is for endless debate rather than definitive scientific solution of problems. Hobbesian optimism on the outcome of social science endeavour was already in eclipse.

Atomistic method spawned atomistic doctrine. The latter rested on twin supports. On the one hand there is what Schumpeter called[5] 'analytic equalitarianism' – the idea that people's faculties of mind and body are about equal in the sense that their variation is so narrowly limited as to make complete equality (and identical functions for utility from income) a permissible working hypothesis. This idea was asserted by Hobbes, in chapter 13 of *Leviathan*, and was espoused by Hooker and by Locke. It is, Schumpeter argued, a pillar of modern analytical economics, yet no serious attempt has been made to verify it.

On the other hand there is the pervasive individualism which presupposes that individuals are logically and ethically prior to society. Here, resistance is encountered from the holistic approach of (*inter alia*) Marxian theory. The debatability of the supposed economic 'axioms' thus begins to emerge. Anthony Giddens notes[6] that:

---

[5] Schumpeter (1954), pp. 121–2.   [6] Giddens (1971), p. 13.

What distinguishes human life from that of animals, according to Marx, is that human faculties, capacities and tastes are shaped by society. The 'isolated individual' is a fiction of utilitarian theory: no human being exists who has not been born into, and thus shaped by, an on-going society.

Third, why *greed*? Because of the dominance of 'associationist' psychology which, from the time of Hobbes, saw the human mind as *tabula rasa*, a slate blank until marked by externally generated sense-impressions. Such forces could be divided into positive and negative categories. On the negative side were pains, repulsions; on the positive were pleasures, satisfactions, desires. As soon as the negative forces had been linked to the cost of supplying goods, and the positive to the utility of consuming them, Hobbes had already assembled the essential features of a utilitarian supply and demand theory of market value.[7]

As hedonistic ideas hardened, they were greeted as an exciting novelty in the eighteenth century. In a celebrated couplet, Alexander Pope exulted:

Oh happiness, Our Being's End and Aim,
Good, Pleasure, Ease, Content, Whate'er thy Name.

Happiness, *bonheur*; hailed, it has been said, by the eighteenth-century philosophers as 'a new word in Europe'. Its novelty reminds us that it does not possess temporal universality at any rate; its coming to prominence in the era of the so-called 'Enlightenment' reminds us that it belongs to the period when theistic Christian faith (that is, faith in the revelation of God's active government of the world) was beginning to decay, being replaced initially by a weak deistic subscription to a providential order of natural law in which the actual and the ideal were indistinguishable.

Thus there was at first no clear distinction between seeking happiness/pleasure/ease/content for oneself, and seeking it for all.[8] Indeed, as Keith Thomas makes plain,[9] the new mid-eighteenth century attitudes of 'benevolence', 'charity', 'tender-heartedness' surfaced first in an entirely new concern for the welfare of animals, and only by analogy were extended to the lower orders of human beings – who perhaps, like animals, possessed feelings? According to Thomas:

[7] Myrdal (1953), pp. 35ff.
[8] Mill (1874) was to make the distinction (chapter 2, paras. 14–16), but to argue that its relevance was restricted to the world's present 'imperfect' state.
[9] Thomas (1983), p. 175.

It was this mode of thought which gave rise to later utilitarianism, for the benevolent, as Cowper [in 'The Task'] put it, wished 'all that were capable of pleasure pleased'.

It is well-known that Adam Smith regarded such multiplication of general utilities as the providential outcome, rather than the objective, of the activity of economic agents. These agents looked to their own interests, and displayed 'insatiability' (greed). Smith, however, in an argument[10] whose subtleties have been largely filtered out of modern economic reasoning:

equated insatiability with 'the corruption of our moral sentiments';

accepted it, however, as the price of a greater (?Rawlsian) good, namely the better satisfaction of the needs of the poor;

attributed it to the fact that people judge their own satisfaction by reference to the positions of those higher or lower than themselves in the rank system of an unequal society;

regarded it as in practice modified by the desire for social esteem (and not only to win such esteem, but to deserve it).

Things move more slowly in Cambridge. A century after Smith, Alfred Marshall was grappling with closely similar issues, as a representative of the Cambridge '1860s generation' seeking to fill the gap left by the post-Darwinian abandonment of even formal Christian belief. Robert Skidelsky is illuminating[11] on Marshall's tortured subtleties as he sought to escape from capitulation to purely egoistic economic motivation. He draws attention to Marshall's conception, partly based on evolutionist ideas, that economic progress would lead to the 'moralisation of wants', because it would be marked by faster growth of 'effort' than of desires; this one might be inclined to interpret as a move in Mill's eudaimonistic direction, were it not that Marshall belonged to the era in which Schumpeter correctly discerned a waning – ultimately seen to be only temporary – of utilitarian faith. Skidelsky also emphasises Marshall's rejection of the exclusive egoism of *homo oeconomicus*, by concentration upon *measurable* motives, in a manner which preserved the professional expertise of calculability after which he hankered, and implicitly assumed that non-measurable motives included some non-egoistic elements.

The hypothesis of measurability of pleasures and pains had, of course, been the contribution of utilitarianism's acknowledged

---

[10] Well described by Hont and Ignatieff (1983).   [11] Skidelsky (1983), chapter 2.

founding father, Jeremy Bentham, with his 'felicific calculus'.[12] It is closely tied up with the notion of rational behaviour to maximise net pleasure, and this leads to the last axiomatic element calling for examination.

Fourth, then, why *rationality* – in the attenuated sense[13] that orthodox economics gives to this term? In the relatively modern economics of the last century or so (following Bentham's earlier lead) it is primarily because of the dominance of stress on pure scientific technique. Increasing doubt about the reliability of knowledge was accompanied by an urge to follow the lead of Descartes and Kant in seeking primarily to discover correct procedures of study: there was a gradual but pervasive shift from supposing that the essence of science resides in taking correct views of the world being examined, to supposing that it resides in the application of correct techniques for study of that elusive reality.

So in economics an ambivalent retreat from confidence in the coherent nature of economic action can be detected, summarised in Boulding's dictum that economists 'do not know what utility is, but cannot do without it'. This retreat was typified by Philip Wicksteed,[14] who proposed to complete Marshall's effective de-ethicising of economic theory by de-psychologising its foundations. Wicksteed proposed to speak of the 'significance' rather than the 'utility' of goods to consumers, and opined that:

There is no occasion to define the economic motive, or the psychology of economic man, for economics studies a type of relation [?between ends and means] not a type of motive.

The ambivalence of the retreat emerged in increasing concern simply to measure correctly the behaviour springing from the undefined motive. F.Y. Edgeworth shared Marshall's and Wicksteed's doubts about utilitarian philosophy, as Keynes made plain.[15]

[12] Though even he was aware that interpersonal comparison of utilities might involve an element of pretence. *Vide* J.G.T. Meeks in Turner and Martin (eds.) (1984), pp. 42–3.

[13] See, for instance, Hahn and Hollis (eds.) (1979), Introduction, p. 12: in Hahn's view 'economics probably made a mistake when it adopted the nomenclature of "rational" when all it meant is correct calculations and an orderly personality'; and Sen (1979), 'Rational Fools' in the same volume, sections VII and VIII: 'A person . . . may be "rational" in the limited sense of revealing no inconsistencies in his choice behaviour, but if he has no use for the distinctions between . . . his interests . . . his welfare . . . his idea of what should be done . . . and . . . his actual choices . . . he must be a bit of a fool'.   [14] Wicksteed (1910).

This did not prevent him from propounding the possibility of measurement of 'utility', in an ordinal though not in a cardinal sense. So we find in his *Mathematical Psychics* the basis of Hicksian indifference analysis of consumer demand:

> We cannot count the golden sands of life; we cannot number the 'innumerable smile' of seas of love; but we seem to be capable of observing that there is here a greater, there a less, multitude of pleasure units, mass of happiness; and that is enough.

But Wicksteed's agnostic rejection of such language concerning the economic maximand eventually prevailed, in the twentieth century's attempted move to a fully behaviourist basis for demand theory, based not on ordinal utility measurement but on Samuelsonian preferences (whose psychology and motivation were no longer to be discussed) revealed in actual market transactions.

However, it is important to notice that proponents of behaviourist methodology in economics do not, indeed cannot, rush into the market place and begin to 'observe' consumers' revealed preferences. Rather the observing mind, as Kant emphasised, plays its necessary active role. What the method does is to construct a conceptual apparatus, a (*qualitative*) framework yielding (quantitatively testable, in principle) predictions – e.g. that quantity demanded will typically vary inversely with price, using two minimal starting assumptions, viz.

(1) that people prefer 'more' to 'less';
(2) that people behave consistently.[16]

For the present purpose, it suffices to note that (1) represents the axiom of private greed, and (2) represents the axiom of private rationality, which is where we came in. Neither (1) nor (2), Little for example concedes, can be 'proved' – because of the 'index number' problem, and because the passage of time brings both new goods and new people. Market theory has no alternative but to assume that the representative consumer, *homo oeconomicus*, behaves thus. Well, axioms are not supposed to need proof. But this brief overview of the historical background helps to show how economists came by them, and underlines the fact that Smith's and Marshall's subtleties were

---

[15] Keynes (1933), Part II, chapter 3.
[16] For the full story, see accounts by Little (1950), chapters 1–3; Robinson (1962), chapter 3; and Robertson (1952), title essay.

lost sight of in the excitement of the twentieth century scientific chase. This fact is a reminder that the un-provable axioms are open to debate, and to this I now turn.

III

Critique

It is frequently claimed for market theory that, however much it may offend against our moral sentiments, it is at least realistic in its view of the behaviour of doubtless imperfect human beings. Economics focusses, it has been said, on the strongest rather than the highest influences on human action. Is not, then, 'private greed' a highly defensible axiomatic assumption for positive economics, whatever difficulties may arise if we wish to follow welfare economics into normative realms? And apologists for market theory also seem willing to defend 'private rationality', often on the grounds that it is necessary to assume its prevalence if rigorous analysis is to proceed. Moreover, sceptics are apt to be confronted with the TINA proposition – There Is No Alternative, save for the Marxian system which our liberal, or would-be liberal, society generally rejects.

The case which I shall be seeking to sketch in this section embraces the propositions that:

(a) even as a view of 'what is', private greed (and its associated variety of rationality) represents at least a seriously incomplete, and arguably an essentially defective, presupposition for the analysis of market activity;

(b) there *is* a non-Marxian alternative view of what is going on in market situations;

(c) recognition and elaboration of this alternative might well take account of the fact that the doctrinal history reviewed in section II above occurred in the course of a process of secularisation in European culture, a process which it can be argued was ill-judged, at least in the sense of having been carried to excessive lengths.

Let us begin, then, to chip away at the existing foundation of economic theory in the supposed realism of private greed rationally pursued. Or, rather, let us resume the chipping away, for critical knockings fortunately never ceased, even during the evolution of liberal orthodoxy. Thus Myrdal (1953) long ago pointed out that, in assuming that the representative agent behaved like *homo oeconomicus*, market theory overlooked its inability to demonstrate that deviations from the fictional creature's behaviour cancelled out, so that it was indeed truly representative.

Even were such a demonstration presumed, however, note that the private greed of *homo oeconomicus*, even on the theory's own terms, is not unproblematic. For private greed is not necessarily synonymous with immediate greed, on account of the impulse to save and to accumulate. It may, thus, be akin to the prudence of Greek Epicureanism, which took the long view of pleasure, rather than to Moore's ideal utilitarianism which stressed the virtues of (un-definable but present) good states of mind, and which partly lay behind J.M. Keynes's effort to de-throne abstinence and saving from their place in the pantheon of Victorian values.[17] That utilitarianism, admittedly in different varieties, can be called in support of the virtues both of future and of present consumption well illustrates its protean plasticity as a philosophical basis for market theory.

Again, the idea of *private* greed is surely rather desperately incomplete. It misses the point, adumbrated by Marx among many others, that greed as a motive force in modern society is as much, arguably more, collective than individual. Western culture has insensibly espoused the goal of 'more, without limits'. Insofar as that goal does characterise individual behaviour, it is arguably a response to pervasive cultural forces rather than to in-built, instinctive impulses.

Further, even secularist thought, when we widen our purview from economics *simpliciter*, recognises that individual behaviour can be viewed differently, facilitating a more complex and realistic picture. Sociologists, for example, often describe the economic behaviour of agents in terms strikingly different from those used by orthodox economic theory. In particular, within the family, people are seen as behaving sacrificially rather than selfishly. Mother in the supermarket sacrifices her own interests to those of her children. Father sticks at a job he hates for the sake of his family. Even if economics responds by shifting its ground to the idea of 'family greed',[18] the apparently

---

[17] Although it was, of course, also an essential element in Keynes's case that present abstinence on the part of consumers would not purchase them enhanced pleasure in the future through enlarged accumulation unless it happened to be matched by an expansionary urge from the entrepreneurs.

[18] And even then it is noticeable that, for instance, Becker (1981, chapter 8) still finds it necessary to exert his ingenuity to show that apparently altruistic behaviour within the family may not be what it so clearly and naturally seems; for if just the head of the household displays altruism, it *could* then be in their own interests for the other family members to behave 'as if' altruists.

minor concession represents a substantial shift in the view presented of what makes human beings tick.[19]

However, this perhaps reluctant collectivism external to the individual needs to be matched by a recognition of the plurality of internal motivation. This is sometimes recognised by economists themselves, as for example in Thomas Schelling's revealingly titled paper 'The intimate contest for self-command'.[20] Economics, says Schelling, is the nearest thing we have to a science of choice; how can it cope with our common private experience of difficulty in doing what we have chosen to do? People behave, sometimes, as if they had two selves – one of which wants, and the other of which does not want, a drink or a Mars bar. Which is the real self – the greedy person, or the one seeking self-control?[21]

Professor Schelling seems unsure of the answer to his own question. The acknowledged founder of his discipline, Adam Smith, was more confident, but perhaps rashly so, when he wrote:[22]

When I endeavour to examine my own conduct, when I endeavour to pass sentence upon it, and either to approve or condemn it, it is evident that, in all such cases, I divide myself, as it were, into two persons . . . [of whom] The first is the spectator, whose sentiments with regard to my own conduct I endeavour to enter into, by placing myself in his situation, and by considering how it would appear to me, when seen from that particular point of view. The second is the agent, the person whom I properly call myself, and of whose conduct, under the character of a spectator, I was endeavouring to form some opinion.

According to Smith, it would seem, the acting individual revealing his market preferences is the real person, but his preferences are likely to be significantly influenced by the internal judge whose views result from sympathetic awareness of the views of external judges in society at large. The internal judge, acting in effect as an impartial spectator, thus provides Smith with a link between collective and individual valuations of economic actions.

For Smith the conscience of the internal judge is in effect *vox populi*. For St Paul, it is surely worth recognising if only for fostering awareness of the range of possible alternatives, conscience is *vox Dei*

---

[19] Sen (1979) has proposed a broader shift away from the self-interest assumption in economics: see below.   [20] Schelling (1980); reprinted in Schelling (1984).

[21] Or again Frank Hahn raises the problems of preferences over alternative selves with his example of the would-be non-smoker. Sen and Williams (eds.) (1982), pp. 191–3.

[22] Smith (1976).

within us. From such a standpoint the internal judge, contrary to Smith's view, is the 'true' self:

I cannot understand my own behaviour. I fail to carry out the things I want to do, and I find myself doing the very things I hate. When I act against my own will, that means I have a self that acknowledges that the Law [of God] is good, and so the thing behaving in that way is not my self but sin living in me.[23]

Moreover, the internal judge is the voice of reason:

I can see that my body follows a . . . law that battles against the law which my reason dictates.[24]

Going back to St Paul might seem impossibly anachronistic to an age which is tempted to identify wisdom with the findings of empirical science dating from the seventeenth century. But it was in Adam Smith's own century that William Law, though writing approvingly of rationality:[25]

Reason is our universal law, that obliges us in all places and at all times; and no actions have any honour, but so far as they are instances of our obedience to reason . . .

gave it this interpretation when applied to greed:[26]

Let us suppose . . . a man to be in love with riches, and to be so eager in pursuit of them, as never to think he has enough: now this passion is so far from supposing any excellent sense, or great understanding, that blindness and folly are the best supports that it hath.

If I am greedy, say St Paul and William Law,[27] it is against my will (a possibility which Schelling understands), and moreover against my reason – rationality and greed are opposites, not correlates. At the very least here we surely see that the modern market theorists' conception of man in his economic sphere is not sacrosanct: there can be other views of the nature of man, as St Paul and William Law, with their very different paradigm, suggest. Neither group, perhaps, should arrogantly claim possession of the whole truth and of all wisdom.[28]

---

[23] Romans, chapter 7, verses 15–17, Jerusalem Bible.
[24] Romans, chapter 7, verse 23.   [25] Law (1729), chapter 14.   [26] Ibid.
[27] Between St Paul and William Law lies a long and highly relevant Christian debate on the nature of true freedom of choice, on which see an extraordinarily perceptive discussion by Ignatieff (1984), chapter 2.
[28] Which, indeed, Christian thought from St Paul onwards does not claim: I Corinthians, chapter 13, verse 12.

Modern utilitarian market theory, it is clear, must plead guilty to the charge of taking at best an exceedingly partial view of human economic motivation. But the situation may be yet more extreme. Some have claimed that the system of market theory is empty of real content and essentially circular in its reasoning. Considerable substance is given to this charge by the confession of Samuelson himself, in his famous textbook, that quite commonly:

the consumer's market behavior is explained in terms of preferences, which are in turn defined only by behavior . . . Often nothing more is stated than the conclusion that people behave as they behave, a theorem which has no empirical implications, since it contains no hypothesis and is consistent with all conceivable behavior, while refutable by none.

The system's possible emptiness also emerges in an example. Lipsey's well-known textbook purported (at least in earlier editions) to elaborate a technical apparatus on a scientific, neutral revealed-preference basis, yet revealed moments of unhappiness at the thought of being either ethically empty or implicitly based on psychological hedonism. So, Lipsey adds a footnote:[29]

It is sometimes argued that in economics individuals are assumed to be narrowly selfish and devoid of any altruistic motives. This is not so. If the individual derives utility from giving his money away to others, this can be incorporated into the analysis [of the attainment of maximum consumer satisfaction from income-use] and we can compare, for example, the marginal utility of a pound that he gives away with the marginal utility of a pound that he spends on himself.

It seems that *sacrificial* giving, of that which in the absence of response to some moral claim we might 'prefer' to spend on ourselves, is for Lipsey impossible; we give – even Mother Teresa toiling in the slums of Bombay – only to maximise our own 'utility'.[30] We are, then, in the position that *either* utility is an umbrella word for '*anything* which moves us to action' – in which case Samuelson is clearly right that it may explain nothing (and further, given the great variety of human motives, there is no particular reason to expect that an economy in which it is the common denominator would exhibit the order and stability to which orthodox liberal economists have a faith-commitment – their key assumption of *consistent* choice would need

[29] Lipsey (1966), p. 182.
[30] This contrasts with the radical approach of Sen to 'commitment', in his paper 'Rational Fools' (1979).

increased justification); *or*, by contrast, utility must indeed represent the own-pleasure principle, whether or not such pleasure arises from the utility of others, and paradoxically even giving is prompted by the final motive of seeking maximum satisfaction for the self. One following Lipsey's line of argument should surely say clearly which of these alternatives is intended: sliding between them fudges the issue. And if the former, more reasonable, option does represent what is meant, then market theory cannot offer much in the way of explanation unless much more is said about what *does* move man to action: economics must as a minimum requirement re-trace its steps to the time when it was recognised as a branch of moral philosophy.

In that latter event, economics students might properly be asked to read a work such as Charles Taylor's *Hegel and Modern Society*, and to become informed on the Kantian revolt against the reductionistic Enlightenment view of man as part of objectified nature, with human motivation to be 'explained causally like all other events', in favour of a view of man as radically free, with a:

Moral freedom which must mean being able to decide against all inclination for the sake of the morally right. This more radical view of course rejected at the same time a utilitarian definition of morality; the morally right could not be determined by happiness and therefore by desire. Instead of being dispersed throughout his diverse desires and inclinations the morally free subject must be able to gather himself together, as it were, and make a decision about his total commitment.

Kant's argument, compatible to some extent with St Paul's and William Law's, is that rational action is something to be achieved by struggling against desires, rather than by yielding to them. Those who regularly yield are in bondage, not freedom. With this wider consciousness, it is time to return to the matter of rationality in its orthodox interpretation, and to note that when it is examined within older and broader frameworks than that of 'relatively modern economics', when (that is) it has any more substance than simple consistency, its dominance is to be explained by (usually utilitarian) acceptance of the notion of *consequentialism*[31] in assessing different modes of behaviour. The main alternative to consequentialism involves attention to the origin of actions rather than to their outcome, and to the principles that might be held to govern right conduct.

[31] Sen and Williams (1982), Introduction.

Consequences versus principles. The disjunction sounds sharp, and I consider first the case for accepting that it *is* sharp.

Consequentialism, according to Professor G.E.M. Anscombe who coined the term, is rooted in philosophical empiricism, whose main tenet is that claims to knowledge can only be justified by experience. We can only experience what *is*, and cannot move (as already argued by David Hume[32]) from 'is' to 'ought'. Therefore we lack any *a priori* principles, and the sheer absence of alternatives forces the conclusion that it is rational to judge behaviour by reference to perceived consequences – as utilitarianism does, the consequences being conceived, in its Benthamite variety, in hedonistic terms.

In sharp contrast to that, the Christian belief is that claims to knowledge can be justified by trust (*rational* trust according to St Paul and to William Law) in God's revelation in Scripture. Therefore we do have 'given' principles. We know what we ought to do in advance of any assessment of the consequences of different kinds of action. Behaviour based on the principles of love, justice, concern for the poor and so on is incumbent upon us. These are not empty slogans, or good things to agree about if only we could find the means to do so, but represent the very substance of the social reality within which we live, for they are the will of the God who created us and to whom we shall one day have to give account. Good hermeneutical procedure, good practice in interpreting scriptural revelation, theologians assure us, consists precisely in eliciting these underlying principles from the biblical text, and then searching for their proper application, as we 'work out our salvation in fear and trembling'.[33]

However, thesis, as usual, meets antithesis. Consequentialism, specifically in utilitarian form, can be presented as not being in sharp conflict with 'principle-ism' at all. For a start, consequences can be emphasised in stronger or in weaker form; as A.K. Sen has said, we can be consequence-sensitive without being consequential*ist* – without, that is, taking the consequences of actions to be the sole determining factor in assessing their worth. Then we may note the existence of quite cogent arguments that utilitarianism can find a place in Christian moral prescription. For example, it can be argued that Mother Teresa is a consequentialist obeying Christian principle. Why sacrifice one's own interests for others? It pays in the end! She is

---

[32] Though in recent years some philosophers, e.g. MacIntyre (1959), have questioned this interpretation of Hume.   [33] Philippians, chapter 2, verse 12.

maximising her eternal rather than her temporal utility ... Or, more generously, she is maximising happiness overall (as in Mill's version of utilitarian principles) at the cost of her own comfort. It might even be argued that Christian principles may form the perfect consequent-ialist code, since they are based not on a limited vision but on an omniscient view of the consequences of action.

And again, Robin Attfield searches[34] for an environmental ethic which does not involve, as some have been wont to argue is necessary, a complete break with previous ethical systems. He finds it in a combination of (a) utilitarianism (in ethical rather than egotistic form – Mill *vice* Bentham?); (b) the Lockean principle on property, that its appropriation to private ownership – by mixing one's labour with it – is permissible, provided that enough is left for other people to follow suit. His argument is that this combination is fully congruent with the Judaeo-Christian principle of stewardship, which can be elicited without any great difficulty from the Old Testament, and applied with (in principle) equal facility to today's problem of environmental protection.

Yet again, others too are taking utilitarianism in a Millian direction, by speaking of the notion of idealisation of preferences.[35] It is argued that we should distinguish, not so much between higher and lower preferences, as between manifest (revealed) and true pre-ferences. The latter are conceived to represent what would be chosen by a rational chooser possessed of full information, on the basis of calm reflection, after the exclusion of such anti-social preferences as sadism, envy, resentment, malice. (There are distinct echoes here of Smith's and Schelling's two choosers in one skin.) The immediate response to this surely has to be that though such laundered preferences could perhaps be relevant to some kinds of economic policy debate, where the political rather than the market element prevails, market theory can only be based on revealed preferences, whatever their character or origin, unless we have a different *kind* of economics, in which principles play an explicit role, and play it *ab initio*, as indeed I propose to argue is desirable.

Even in the political sphere, utilitarianism *simpliciter* can be dangerous. Charles Taylor, for example, cites[36] Hegel's argument

---

[34] Attfield (1983), pp. 98–110.
[35] Sen and Williams (eds.) (1982), Introduction, and paper by Harsanyi.
[36] Taylor (1979), pp. 101–2.

that it can too easily step over the brink in which man becomes a means and not an end, as for instance with 'reforms' like the English Poor Law of 1834, which put the unemployed into workhouses for the sake of general utility; such obliquity arises from utilitarianism's lack of any notion of intrinsic good. Pursuing such themes, Taylor argues that in the political realm it is now clear that 'the utilitarian perspective is no less an ideology than its major rivals, and no more plausible'.

In the economic sphere I suggest that utilitarian ideology, in the narrow market-oriented revealed preference form that in fact prevails, simply fails to grapple with the realities of the human situation. Then economics as a properly social, that is to say a human, science is betrayed through a built-in allegiance to the essentially unrestrained market economy. We witness a mutually reinforcing process of what has been called economism, of exaggeration of the domain and application of the economic (narrowly conceived) in theory and in practice. As to theory, note the process of cultural imperialism by which economists seek to explain, not only economic behaviour, but also political behaviour[37] and family behaviour,[38] using the fundamental economic model of constrained, self-interested utility maximisation. As to practice, take cognisance of the argument by Fred Hirsh[39] that there is a 'commercialization bias' inherent in modern economic growth; this bias Hirsch argues to represent excessive extensive use of the market, which can be seen to be paralleled[40] by excessive *int*ensive use of the market, as features that arise from healthy continuing relationships between specific individuals and groups are regarded as reflecting sub-optimal cross-subsidisation, to be eliminated on efficiency grounds.

These issues raise the question, treated by Robin Matthews,[41] of the proper limits to the market, limits which – given the costs and inherent inadequacy of legal regulation – need, *even for efficiency*, to partake of a moral character. The trouble, as Matthews candidly recognises, is that secular thought cannot readily delineate an acceptable moral framework for the modern world (in which Adam Smith's version of pressure from public opinion is ineffective, probably because of the impersonality and anonymity of modern society). Commercial morality, based on honesty and trust, is too

---

[37] Downs (1957).   [38] Becker (1981).   [39] Hirsch (1977).
[40] Cramp (forthcoming), section VIII.   [41] Matthews (1981).

limited a conception. The Kantian categorical imperative is too demanding both of moral resources and of knowledge of the effects of different actions. Complete altruism can prevent solutions emerging at all; and restricted altruism (altruism in redistribution combined with egoism in market dealings) is of too schizophrenic a character to guide the actions of human beings whose behaviour is marked, *inter alia*, by a craving for unity and coherence.

Thoughtful writers here seem to share some despair at the difficulty in framing an explicit ethical principle to guide us, in a manner which narrowly economic utilitarianism has clearly failed to do. But they generally do not consider one that is already to hand, if we seek to develop an ethic out of our neglected traditions,[42] and attempt consistent development of themes to which lip-service has long been paid in western culture. Within that culture, I am convinced that the guidance needed comes from the tradition of Christian moral philosophy rather than from the tradition of mechanistic physical-social science.[43]

In its strong form, an economics congruent with Christian moral philosophy[44] begins by recognising that God as creator is the *alpha* and *omega* of all human activity, including economic activity. The latter represents, then, the use of God-given *means* to attain God-ordained *ends*.

As to means, man is not owner but steward. For example, the Old Testament law (Leviticus, chapter 25) on the holding of land, then the principal productive asset, makes clear that it is not to be excessively exploited (the sabbath year of rest), and moreover cannot be permanently alienated (the Jubilee provision, against excessive concentration of productive wealth); man has only a limited, authorised, jurisdiction.

As to ends, man's trusteeship is essentially collective – so that, even though the land is allocated to specific (extended) family groups, its use calls for acceptance of responsibilities to fellow-men, instanced in the provision for tithes, gleanings and so on (Deuteronomy, chapters 14, 23, 26 . . .).

---

[42] Attfield (1983), p. 4.
[43] J.S. Mill's comparatively subtle, though perhaps not fully self-consistent, version of utilitarianism may well have more in common with the former tradition than with the latter; but it is the latter that has served as the usual model for utilitarian economics.
[44] Storkey (1979), chapters 13–14; Goudzwaard (1979), chapter 19.

We can, then, following Goudzwaard, begin to discern the implications of the principle or norm of stewardship for the economic sphere, by seeing it as the socially rewarding disposition of the economic resources entrusted to man's care. These 'resources' are to be conceived in a broad sense, as means of production embracing natural resources, human energy and skills, biological life; we are not to restrict ourselves, in the Cartesian tradition and the orthodox economics spawned by it, to what can be quantified and what (often much the same thing in practice) can command a price in the market.

What difference does it make? The flavour of the answer can be indicated by taking as an example the treatment by orthodox and by stewardly economics of the concept of profit or surplus, which is clearly of central importance to any type of economic model or analytical framework. Surplus is defined by Goudzwaard as 'the attainment of a positive balance between economic results and economic sacrifices', where these are widely defined to cover both market and non-market resources. It is thus the sign of a positive answer to the economic norm of stewardship. It is an essential element in the operation of healthy undertakings; an enterprise ceases to be 'economic' (stewardly) if it cannot (in the long run) accumulate a surplus between the quantum of real needs satisfied and the sacrifice of (market plus non-market) resources.

Note the contrast with a typical orthodox economic definition of profit[45] as

the excess of revenues over opportunity costs, whatever the source of such excess,

where 'revenues' refers to total money revenues in the ordinary accounting sense; and 'opportunity costs' refers to total money costs in an accounting sense, but adjusted to give 'economic' profit by adding the monetary return which the capital and managerial talent could have earned in their most profitable alternative uses. Essentially the same 'rational maximising behaviour' would be required to attain an optimum position, whether profit be conceived in this orthodox economic, or in the mere accounting, sense: both look to a maximising of the gap between monetary revenues and costs, *whatever the source* of such excess.

In concentrating on the monetary excess, and eschewing consideration of its source, the orthodox approach invites un-noticed

---

[45] Lipsey (1966), p. 252.

contraventions of the norm of stewardship. Profit, on the prevalent conception, is but a shadow of a responsibly created surplus. One can point to three main elements of profit which would be excluded from a stewardly conception of surplus:

(1) elements arising from externalities, for example the social costs of pollution;

(2) elements arising from the exploitation of market power, for example in particular elements resulting from marketing effort and sales promotion to persuade consumers to buy 'goods' which are not really needed, and may in various ways be positively damaging to individual or collective interests;

(3) elements resulting from the violation in the industrial enterprise of *non-economic* norms – we may instance bad working conditions, boring jobs which do not contribute to (and may often derogate from) the use and development of workers' true gifts and powers, subsistence wages which do not permit workers' families to fulfil their calling *qua* families.

But it will of course immediately strike attention that this three-fold listing is not entirely foreign to the concerns of orthodox economics, at least in some of its manifestations. I have in fact arranged the categories in descending order of relevance conceded by (more or less) orthodox thought. Category (1) has indeed been of major concern to orthodox, secular thinkers in recent decades, but there is weakness in their attempt to deal with it essentially as an after-thought adjustment to the results of a market activity presumed to be benign until strong contrary evidence is provided. Category (2) is a matter of considerable debate among orthodox economists, but they again find difficulty in reaching agreement because their formal apparatus of analysis presumes the acceptability of business behaviour that is validated by market success.

Category (3), however, is virtually excluded from the purview of standard economics, though not from that of sociology – which, however, offers relatively little by way of incisive discussion of the phenomena and their remedies. It has been much discussed by economic historians, for it was perhaps in the earlier phases of the Industrial Revolution that non-economic norms were most consistently violated,[46] and that matters would most obviously have proceeded differently had moral evaluation of economic activity not become so attenuated by quasi-scientific, mechanistic ideas.

[46] Goudzwaard (1979), pp. 65–6.

It is also of interest to note[47] that the principle enunciated under category (3) can be seen as in keeping with a principle discussed in recent social philosophy by John Rawls. There appears to be some analogy between the form of the argument above and that of the one Rawls brings to bear against classical utilitarianism in, for instance, sections VI and VII of his paper 'Justice as fairness'.[48] Rawls here relates his title to the assessment of the institution of slavery, arguing that – in contrast with classical utilitarianism –

the conception of justice as fairness . . . would not allow one to consider that advantages of the slaveholder . . . The question whether these gains outweigh the disadvantages to the slave and to society cannot arise, since in considering the justice of slavery these gains have no weight at all which requires that they be overridden.

The argument here advanced may be regarded as showing that even wider use than Rawls's can (indeed should) be made of the general idea that some changes in profit or in utility, conventionally regarded as gains, cannot be counted as gains *at all* (to be offset against associated costs), since they arise from the violation of certain basic principles – in the case of the present argument, of norms (including but not restricted to the norm of justice) relating to other spheres of life, which it is illegitimate to infringe in pursuit of the economic norm.

These are not matters which economists can cheerfully leave to be considered by other disciplines. Rather, they belong fairly and squarely in the economic sphere. Market profit, in the light of the *economic* norm of stewardship, is seen to be an inadequate guide to economic activity. Competition between producers directed towards the accumulation of a stewardly surplus is acceptable. Competition directed towards the destruction of competitors, and to the exploitation of non-economic spheres of life by using them as instruments in the competitive struggle, is not acceptable. It would be excluded from adoption by producers trained to consider their activity, from start to finish, in the context of the principle of stewardship. That self-discipline could be reinforced by community regulation in an economic and social order based on Christian principles.

Pursuing the argument where it leads, I have gradually moved from

---

[47] As has been pointed out to me by the editor of the present volume, who has also made numerous other suggestions serving to improve the content as well as the form of this paper.   [48] Rawls (1962).

focus on consumption, following the lead of orthodox economics, to focus on production. That is significant, for it is in the basic orientation of seeing supposedly endlessly greedy consumers as sovereign, and production as purely instrumental to the utilitarian satisfaction of consumer desires, that orthodox economics is most grievously distorted. The doctrine of consumer sovereignty prevents it from perceiving clearly that, in the unrestrained market economy, consumers – far from being free and sovereign choosers – are closer to being the helpless victims of an economic process whose motor is technical change (not automatically 'progress'), and whose transmission mechanism is to be discovered in sales pressures by producers and social pressures from fellow-consumers, as one new goody after another spreads through society on the 'infectious disease' model. Moreover, its doctrine of purely instrumental production prevents it from perceiving the real nature of employment, for those very same less-than-sovereign consumers are also people for whom work, far from being a mere utilitarian pain, is absolutely necessary to personal development and fulfilment.

I believe that all honest social science begins from 'I believe', and that if enthusiastic market economists honestly re-examined their (usually only implicit) beliefs about the human condition, they would have good reason to be appalled.

References
Attfield, R. (1983), *The Ethics of Environmental Concern*, Oxford: Basil Blackwell.
Becker, G.S. (1981), *A Treatise on the Family*, Cambridge, Mass.: Harvard University Press.
Cramp, A.B., *Economics in Christian Perspective: A Sketch-Map*, forthcoming.
Downs, A. (1957), *An Economic Theory of Democracy*, New York: Harper and Row.
Giddens, A. (1971), *Capitalism and Modern Social Theory*, Cambridge University Press.
Goudzwaard, B. (1979), *Capitalism and Progress*, Toronto: Wedge Publishing Foundation.
Hahn, F.H. (1982), 'On Some Difficulties of the Utilitarian Economist', in A.K. Sen and B. Williams (eds.).
Hahn, F.H. and Hollis, M. (eds.) (1979), *Philosophy and Economic Theory*, Oxford: Clarendon Press.
Harsanyi, J.C. (1982), 'Morality and the Theory of Rational Behaviour', in A.K. Sen and B. Williams (eds.).

Hirsch, F. (1977), *Social Limits to Growth*, London: Routledge and Kegan Paul.

Hont, I. and Ignatieff, M. (1983), 'Needs and Justice in the Wealth of Nations: An Introductory Essay', in I. Hont and M. Ignatieff (eds.), *Wealth and Virtue*, Cambridge University Press.

Ignatieff, M. (1984), *The Needs of Strangers*, London: Chatto and Windus.

Keynes, J.M. (1933), *Essays in Biography*, London: R. Hart-Davis.

Law, W. (1729), *A Serious Call to a Devout and Holy Life*, London: W. Innys.

Little, I.M.D. (1950), *A Critique of Welfare Economics*, Oxford: Clarendon Press.

Lipsey, R.G. (1966), *An Introduction to Positive Economics*, 2nd Edition, London: Weidenfeld and Nicolson.

MacIntyre, A.C. (1959), 'Hume on "is" and "ought"', *Philosophical Review*, 68: 451–68.

Matthews, R.C.O. (1981), 'Morality, Competition and Efficiency', *The Manchester School*, 49: 289–309.

Meeks, J.G.T. (1984), 'Utility in Economics: A Survey of the Literature', in C.F. Turner and E. Martin (eds.), *Surveying Subjective Phenomena*, Vol. 2, New York: Russell Sage Foundation.

Mill, J.S. (1874), *Utilitarianism*, 5th edition, London: Longmans Green Reader and Dyer.

Mini, P.V. (1974), *Philosophy and Economics*, Gainseville: University Presses of Florida.

Myrdal, G. (1953), *The Political Element in the Development of Economic Theory*, translated by P. Streeten, London: Routledge and Kegan Paul.

Rawls, J. (1962), 'Justice as Fairness', in P. Laslett and W.G. Runciman (eds.), *Philosophy, Politics and Society*, Second Series, chapter 7, Oxford: Basil Blackwell.

Robertson, D.H. (1952), *Utility and All That*, London: George Allen & Unwin.

Robinson, J. (1962), *Economic Philosophy*, London: C.A. Watts & Co.

Schelling, T. (1980), 'The Intimate Contest for Self-Command', *The Public Interest*, 60: 94–118.

(1984), *Choice and Consequence: Perspectives of an Errant Economist*, Cambridge, Mass.: Harvard University Press.

Schumpeter, J.S. (1954), *History of Economic Analysis*, New York: Oxford University Press.

Sen, A.K. (1979), 'Rational Fools: A Critique of the Behavioural Foundations of Economic Theory', in F.H. Hahn and M. Hollis (eds.).

Sen, A.K. and Williams, B. (eds.) (1982), *Utilitarianism and Beyond*, Cambridge University Press.

Skidelsky, R. (1983), *John Maynard Keynes, Volume 1: Hopes Betrayed 1883–1920*, London: Macmillan.

Smith, A. (1976), *The Theory of Moral Sentiments*, edited by D.D. Raphael and A.L. Macfie, Oxford: Clarendon Press (First Edition, 1759).

Storkey, A. (1979), *A Christian Social Perspective*, Leicester: Inter Varsity Press.

Taylor, C. (1979), *Hegel and Modern Society*, Cambridge University Press.

Thomas, K. (1983), *Man and the Natural World*, London: Allen Lane.

Wicksteed, P.H. (1910), *The Common Sense of Political Economy*, London: Macmillan.

6 Rationality and the sure-thing principle*

JOHN BROOME

I

Rationality constrains preferences. If a person is to be rational her preferences must conform to certain requirements. Amongst them are requirements of internal coherence or consistency. These coherence requirements are generally expressed by means of axioms. Some of the axioms are controversial: there is disagreement about whether they really are requirements of rationality. At the moment there is disagreement about the axiom known as 'the strong independence axiom' or, in the version I shall be concerned with,[1] 'the sure-thing principle'. My own belief is that this axiom is genuinely a requirement of rationality; to be rational a person must conform to it. The objections that have been made to it do raise a problem, which I shall consider in section X, but it is not a problem with this axiom. The purpose of this paper is to justify my belief. But, since the sure-thing principle is complicated and applies only to preferences amongst alternatives that involve some uncertainty, it will be useful to discuss a simpler aspect of coherence first. This will help to clarify what is at issue.

Since 'prefer' has an elastic meaning, I must declare from the start that I shall use it only in the sense that satisfies:

* While I was working on this paper (completed in the spring of 1985) I was lucky enough to hear Amartya Sen present his 'Rationality and Uncertainty' at the University of Bath, and to discuss it with him afterwards. This was very useful to me. Readers will recognise many parallels in our argument, though our conclusions are different. I have also learnt a lot from conversations with Susan Hurley about her (1985) paper 'Supervenience and the Possibility of Coherence', and from the extremely helpful comments sent me by Ellery Eells, Ole Hagen, John Harsanyi, Adam Morton, Robert Sugden and Lee Tien. The arguments of this essay are developed further in my *Weighing Goods* (1991), chapter 5.

[1] Savage's (1972), pp. 21–4.

PC: '*N* prefers *A* to *B*' implies 'If *N* were to have a choice between *A* and *B* only, she would choose *A*'.

PC does not define 'prefer' because the implication goes only one way, but it fixes its sense tightly enough for my purposes.

There are some choices that a person cannot possibly be faced with. For instance, a person can never have a choice between remembering a debt and unintentionally forgetting it. Sometimes the impossibility may be causal rather than, as in this example, logical. I shall be needing this definition:

N has a *practical preference* between *A* and *B* if and only if she has a preference between *A* and *B* and it is possible for her to have a choice between *A* and *B* only.

Even non-practical preferences may satisfy *PC*. It may well be true that if a person did have a choice between remembering a debt and unintentionally forgetting it – she cannot, but if she could – she would choose to forget unintentionally. The subjunctive conditional in *PC* can extend this far.

II

To begin with let us look at preferences amongst alternatives that contain no uncertainty. The principal coherence axiom for preferences like these is transitivity: if a person prefers *A* to *B* and *B* to *C* she should, to be rational, prefer *A* to *C*.[2]

Before considering the transitivity of preferences, I need to settle what sort of thing people have preferences between. I am going to take preferences to be between *propositions*. Often we speak of preferences between objects or classes of objects. I prefer Oxford to Colchester and Volkswagens to Fiats. But these preferences can always be redescribed as preferences between propositions. I prefer 'I visit Oxford' to 'I visit Colchester' and 'I own a Volkswagen' to 'I own a Fiat'. Taking preferences to be between propositions permits perfect generality.

[2] Coherence is normally taken to require the existence of a preference quasi-ordering. This implies also that indifference should be transitive and reflexive. Sugden's (1985) discussion of coherence is conducted in terms of a weaker condition, defined on choice functions rather than binary preferences. I have chosen to deal with transitivity of preference because it is the most familiar condition, but what I shall be saying applies equally to other related conditions.

A precedent is Richard Jeffrey's decision theory.[3] But I am not going to adopt the whole of Jeffrey's scheme. Jeffrey assumes that people have preferences between propositions that are not mutually exclusive. But, in keeping with most theories of choice, I am going to suppose that preferences are between mutually exclusive alternatives, which together exhaust all the possibilities. This means that the field of preferences will be a set of contrary (mutually exclusive) propositions, whose disjunction is necessarily true. So one and only one of these propositions will be true. Each of them I shall call a 'possibility'.

How are possibilities to be individuated? A proposition can be thought of as a class of possible worlds, the worlds in which the proposition is true. The field of preference, conceived this way, will be a partition of all possible worlds into disjoint classes. How is the classification to be made? Of two possible worlds, what determines whether they should be classed together in one possibility or separately in two? What differences between worlds are enough to separate them?

III

A natural idea to start off with is that we should individuate possibilities as finely as we can, and take any differences at all as enough to separate one world from another. If two worlds differ in any respect – if there is any proposition that is true in one and false in the other – we should classify them in different possibilities. But this proposal runs into a snag. If we individuate this finely, the requirement of transitivity loses its bite. It does not constrain preferences at all in any way that could be practically significant.

Before I explain this in general it is worth having an example. George prefers visiting Rome to mountaineering in the Alps, and he prefers staying at home to visiting Rome. However, if he were to have a choice between staying at home and mountaineering in the Alps, he would choose to go mountaineering. In the sense given by *PC*, then, he does not prefer staying at home to mountaineering. But George claims to be rational and denies that his preferences are intransitive. Where we distinguished only three possibilities, mountaineering, visiting Rome and staying at home, George distinguishes four:

[3] Jeffrey (1983).

M = George goes mountaineering
R = George visits Rome
H_1 = George does not reject a mountaineering trip and George stays at home
H_2 = George rejects a mountaineering trip and George stays at home.

(He is willing to distinguish more, but these are enough for his argument.) George prefers R to M and H_1 to R. He agrees that transitivity requires him to prefer H_1 to M. But, he points out, if he were to have a choice between mountaineering and staying at home, that would be a choice between M and H_2. And nothing requires him to prefer H_2 to M.

To generalise George's point, consider a person who has a practical preference (either way) between possibilities A and B. Since the preference is practical it is possible for this person to have a choice between A and B only, and if she does it must be possible for her to choose B. If she did have this choice, and if she chose B, it would then be the case that:

(1) The person had a choice between A and B only, and chose B

This proposition would be true in the world that resulted from her choice. Since she would have chosen B, the possibility B must include this world. If, then, we individuate worlds so finely that no two worlds are classified in the same possibility unless they are the same in every respect, no world can be included in B unless (1) is true in that world. But such a world can only result from the person's having a choice between A and B only and choosing B. If we individuate this finely, then, the same possibility can never be one of the alternatives in different choices. It is not possible for our person to have a choice between B and any other possibility besides A. So she cannot have a practical preference between B and any other possibility besides A. If, to summarise, a person has a practical preference between two possibilities, she cannot have a practical preference between either of them and any third possibility.

It follows that, if we individuate to the finest degree, practical preferences are not constrained at all by transitivity. Transitivity requires that if A is preferred to B and B to C, then A must be preferred to C. But it can never be the case that A is practically preferred to B and B practically preferred to C. So amongst practical preferences the requirement of transitivity is vacuously satisfied.

A person may, of course, have non-practical preferences. Indeed, supposing still that we are individuating to the finest degree, she must have if her preferences are to be complete. If she has a preference between A and B, her preference between B and any third alternative must be non-practical. George in our example has not individuated quite to the finest degree but even so he has non-practical preferences. For instance, he prefers H_1, staying at home without having rejected a mountaineering trip, to M, mountaineering. If he could have a choice between H_1 and M – if rather than mountaineering, he could stay at home and somehow rub out his rejection of mountaineering – that is what he would do. But this is not a possible choice.

Transitivity certainly imposes restrictions on a person's complete pattern of preferences including non-practical ones. Since George prefers H_1 to R to M he must prefer H_1 to M. But if we individuate possibilities to the finest degree, practical preferences will be only a small subset of all preferences, and transitivity allows them to have any pattern at all. Practical preferences, however, are the only ones that can directly determine a choice. So transitivity will have been robbed of its practical significance.

IV

What should we do about this? To help the discussion along I shall say something more about George. He has some reasons for his preferences. Mountaineering frightens him, so he prefers visiting Rome. Sightseeing bores him, so he prefers to stay at home. But to decide to stay at home when he could have gone mountaineering strikes him as cowardly. (To decide to visit Rome when he could have gone mountaineering strikes him as cultured, not cowardly.)

Is George rational? I am not so unwise as to venture an opinion on this, but I shall try to sort out what the question turns on. George distinguishes the possibility H_1 from H_2, and his claim to rationality is that these two possibilities do not have to occupy the same place in his preference ordering. Although he must prefer H_1 to M, he believes he need not prefer H_2 to M. Actually his preferences in descending order are: H_1, R, M, H_2. George's claim is that it is rational for him to have a preference between H_1 and H_2, and we now know the basis of that claim: one involves a cowardly decision and the other does not.

Since we are taking preferences to be between possibilities and since we are looking for some understanding of rational preferences, it is obvious that we must individuate possibilities at least as finely as is needed to represent any preference that is rational. If, then, it is really rational for George to have a preference between H_1 and H_2, we must certainly count them as different possibilities. If we do, transitivity will not constrain George to prefer staying at home to mountaineering, and we can agree that he is rational. The question is whether, actually, H_1 and H_2 do differ enough to make it rational for him to prefer one to the other. George believes that one involves a cowardly decision and the other does not. Let us assume for the sake of argument (I shall say more about this in section V) that if this is true it is indeed rational for George to prefer one to the other. So the only question left is whether it really would be cowardly for George to turn down a mountaineering trip and stay at home instead.

It is never a possibility that George might be rational and at the same time not have transitive preferences. If it would be rational for George to choose to go mountaineering rather than to stay at home, that can only be because it is rational for him to distinguish H_2 from H_1 and prefer one to the other. His preferences are then transitive. There can only be an appearance of rational intransitivity if we individuate possibilities coarsely and at the same time allow fine distinctions to determine what is rational: if in the example we insist that staying at home is only a single possibility, but allow that preferences between staying at home and other alternatives might rationally depend on whether or not staying at home involves a cowardly choice. But if fine distinctions can affect rational preferences we must also allow them to individuate possibilities. Otherwise we shall have a rational preference between a possibility and itself, and this is nonsense.

Suppose for a moment that George is wrong and the difference between H_1 and H_2 is not enough to justify a preference between them. George's preferences are not then rational (fully – I shall say more in section V about partial rationality). But what sort of irrationality do they suffer from? The natural thing to say is that they are incoherent, intransitive in fact, because George prefers visiting Rome to mountaineering, and staying at home to visiting Rome, but he does not prefer staying at home to mountaineering. But so long as we continue to distinguish H_1 from H_2 George is definitely not guilty of intransitivity. He can only be convicted of this charge if we deny that H_1 and H_2 are different possibilities.[4] And that is the right thing

---

[4] Alternatively we might insist that H_1 and H_2 must be indifferent to each other. I shall mention this alternative below.

to do. Worlds must be classified in different possibilities if they differ in a way that could justify a preference. But if they do not, then we should classify them in the same possibility. That way we shall give the requirement of transitivity just the right force. We shall count as intransitive precisely those preferences that ought to be counted as intransitive, and no more.

So this is the principle I recommend for individuating possibilities: worlds should be classified in different possibilities if and only if they differ in a way that can justify a preference. Some propositions justify a preference and others do not; let us call them 'justifiers' and 'non-justifiers' respectively. An example of a justifier, I have been assuming, is:

(2) George makes a cowardly decision.

And I have been assuming that:

(3) George rejects mountaineering in favour of staying at home

is an example of a non-justifier. It is not by itself enough to justify a preference. It is true in H_2 and false in H_1, but only if proposition (2) or some other justifier is also true in H_2 and false in H_1 is a preference between them justified. My proposal is that worlds should be classified into possibilities by means of justifiers only. If some justifier is true in one world and false in another, the two worlds must be placed in different possibilities. But if two worlds differ only in the truth-values of non-justifiers they must be placed in the same possibility.

There is an alternative to this scheme of individuation that would serve the same purpose. We might individuate possibilities as finely as we like, perhaps allowing any proposition to differentiate them, but at the same time supplement the requirements of coherence with some rational principles of indifference. Rationality, we should say, requires a person to be indifferent between possibilities that differ only in the truth-values of non-justifiers. Actually this would be a more satisfactory scheme in some ways. The scheme I have suggested has the awkwardness that it does not allow some irrational preferences to be recognised as preferences at all. Even if H_1 and H_2 do not differ in any justifier, George might irrationally have a preference between them. But in my scheme they will not be recognised as different possibilities, so this preference cannot be expressed. The classification of possibilities in my scheme implicitly embodies principles of rationality, so it cannot accommodate certain sorts of irrationality. In the alternative scheme these principles are made explicit. Nevertheless, in this paper, which is concerned with rational preferences only, I think the awkwardness is tolerable. I have adopted my scheme because it fits into existing decision theory much more easily. Decision theory has traditionally individuated possibilities rather coarsely, and its axioms are inconvenient to use with a very fine individuation. My scheme also follows the precedent of earlier discussions about the individuation of alternatives.[5]

My scheme does, of course, assume implicitly the existence of the principles of rationality that would be explicit in the alternative scheme: a rational person must be indifferent between classes of worlds that differ only in non-justifiers. It is quite a common opinion that the only principles of rationality are the requirements of coherence.[6] This amounts to denying the existence of non-justifiers. According to this view, any difference between alternatives is enough to justify a preference. George, in pointing out that H_1 and H_2 differ in the truth-value of proposition (3) above, sufficiently justifies his preference between them. In this section and the last I have explained the very severe penalty attached to this view. If we do not accept that a proposition like (3) or even (1) is a non-justifier, then we shall be forced to accept that transitivity does not in any way constrain practical preferences. If, to put it another way, coherence were really the only requirement of rationality, then coherence itself would require nothing of practical preferences. I hope I may assume that rationality must impose *some* conditions on practical preferences. At the very least, then, rationality cannot allow propositions like (1) to justify a preference. So there must be some propositions that are non-justifiers; there must be some rational principles of indifference.

The difficult thing, of course, is to decide what these principles are. Which propositions are justifiers and which are not? To settle this properly one would need a theory of the foundations of rationality, which I do not propose to supply. Fortunately, though, my argument will not require it. If a theory is to constrain practical preference it

---

[5] For instance: Drèze (1974), p. 15, Eells (1982), pp. 39–40, 75–6, MacCrimmon and Larsson (1979), pp. 397–8, Machina (1981), p. 173, Samuelson (1966), p. 136, Tversky (1967), p. 198; (1975), pp. 170–3.

[6] Allais (1979, p. 70): 'There are no criteria for the rationality of ends as such other than the condition of consistency'. It is odd that Allais should hold this opinion and at the same time insist on individuating possibilities very coarsely. See section VII.

must acknowledge some non-justifiers. I shall insist on that, but otherwise I shall be neutral between competing theories. The second thing I shall insist on is that, whatever one's theory, and whatever propositions one may count as justifiers, those propositions must be used to individuate possibilities. If two worlds differ in a justifier, they must be classified in different possibilities. The penalty for disobeying this rule is to find oneself talking nonsense: saying that a possibility might rationally be preferred to itself.

V

In this section I shall mention a few alternative views about what propositions are justifiers, because they will come up later. I am not, remember, taking sides on them myself.

One common view is that a person's good and bad feelings are justifiers for that person. Suppose that in one of two alternatives a person feels fear, anxiety, regret, exhilaration, pleasure or some other good or bad feeling, and in the other she feels it to a different degree or not at all. According to this view it would be rational for her to prefer one to the other.

There are some grounds for arguing that *irrational* feelings should not be included as justifiers. Doing so may force us to distinguish possibilities that ought not to be distinguished. Let us go back to George. Suppose, for the sake of argument, that it would actually not be cowardly for him to stay at home instead of going mountaineering, and there is nothing else to justify a preference between H_1 and H_2. Then according to my recommended scheme, H_1 and H_2 should be included in the same possibility. Transitivity then requires George to prefer staying at home to mountaineering. But suppose George, irrational though it is,[7] will lose some of his self-respect if he stays at home. Then, if we accept irrational feelings as justifiers, we shall have to recognise H_1 and H_2 as genuinely different possibilities; in one George loses some of his self-respect and in the other he does not. Transitivity, then, will lose its grip once more. It will no longer

---

[7] George might either believe falsely that to stay at home is cowardly, or else be emotionally influenced by such a view even though he recognises it as false. If he has the false belief we might not normally call him irrational, either in having the belief or in having the feelings that result from it. We do not normally consider a person irrational for having a false belief unless she has good evidence that it is false. So in talking about irrational feelings here I am extending the meaning of 'irrational' to include feelings that a rational person would not have if she had true beliefs.

constrain George to prefer staying at home to mountaineering. So it seems as though, by accepting irrational feelings as justifiers, we once more free practical preferences from the constraints of coherence.

But I do not think this is correct. Suppose we do take irrational feelings as justifiers. Even so, given that no cowardice is involved, rationality definitely requires George to prefer staying at home to mountaineering. He cannot escape this requirement and still be rational. Certainly, if he is liable to lose his self-respect it is rational for him to take this into account. But he is still irrational to some extent in being in this position. And furthermore, it is only rational for George to take into account feelings that he will actually have. We only have to distinguish H_1 from H_2 if George actually will lose some of his self-respect by choosing to stay at home rather than go mountaineering. This, in the partial sense I have described, frees George from the constraints of transitivity. But generally when transitivity imposes a constraint George will not have any irrational feelings to release him from it.

I think it is a tenable view, then, that irrational feelings should be included as justifiers. But I do not insist on it.

Another view is that a person may rationally prefer one alternative to another if anybody's feelings, not just her own, differ in the two alternatives in a way that is good or bad. Anybody's feelings are justifiers for anybody. Against this must be set the theory that rationality requires self-interest. This theory I believe to have been discredited,[8] but, once again, in this paper I need not insist on this.

It may also be thought that other differences between alternatives, besides feelings, may justify a preference. Against this must be set the utilitarian tradition. Traditional utilitarians believe that ultimately only people's feelings matter, and only they can justify a preference. This has been argued over a lot,[9] and again I shall not take sides here. I do want to say, though, that the possibility of justifiers other than feelings must be taken seriously. I shall be giving a plausible example of one later, and in fact I have already given one. Suppose, to reverse our latest assumption, that it actually would be cowardly for George to turn down a mountaineering trip in order to stay at home. Then, I assumed earlier, it would be rational for him to prefer H_1 to H_2. The difference that justifies this preference is that H_2 involves a cowardly

---

[8] Most thoroughly in Parfit (1984).
[9] For a recent discussion see Griffin (1986).

choice and H_1 does not. This is not a difference in feelings. We may suppose, to purify the example, that the alternatives do not differ in feelings at all. Suppose that as soon as George has made his choice he will for some reason – perhaps a drug – forget what alternative he has rejected. It is plausible that, even so, George might rationally prefer H_1 to H_2. It seems rational to want to avoid acting in a cowardly way, whatever the effect on one's feelings might be.

VI

Now I come to uncertainty. I shall take preferences to be between 'gambles' over possibilities, though in section X I shall recommend a different assumption. A typical gamble will be: possibility A_1 if S_1 occurs, A_2 if S_2 occurs, . . . A_n if S_n occurs. S_1 . . . S_n are mutually exclusive and exhaustive 'states of nature', which I take to be statistically independent of a person's choices amongst gambles. I am, then, adopting a simplified version of Savage's system, with a slightly different terminology.[10]

Once uncertainty is taken into account the principal coherence axiom in decision theory is, in Savage's version, the 'sure-thing principle' (STP). It goes like this. Let the n states of nature be arbitrarily partitioned into two groups: S_1 . . . S_r and S_{r+1} . . . S_n. Suppose there are four gambles of the form shown in table 6.1. For each gamble that may be chosen and each state that may occur the table shows which possibility will result. The STP says that if a person prefers F_1 to F_2 she must, to be rational, prefer G_1 to G_2.[11]

For convenience I shall write $W(F_1, S_i)$ to stand for the world that would come about – all that would be the case – if F_1 were chosen rather than F_2 and S_i were to occur, $W(F_2, S_i)$ for the world that would come about if F_2 were chosen rather than F_1 and S_i were to occur, $W(G_1, S_i)$ for the world that would come about if G_1 were chosen rather than G_2 and S_i were to occur, and $W(G_2, S_i)$ for the world that would come about if G_2 were chosen rather than G_1 and S_i were to occur. Table 6.1 shows that $W(F_1, S_1)$ is a member of the possibility A_1, $W(G_1, S_n)$ a member of D_n, and so on.

[10] Savage (1972). Unlike Savage I am assuming a finite number of states of nature, but this is merely for ease of writing. My 'possibilities' are Savage's 'consequences'. My 'gambles' are Savage's 'acts'.

[11] It also says that if she is indifferent between F_1 and F_2 she must be indifferent between G_1 and G_2.

Table 6.1

		States of nature			
		$S_1 \ldots S_r$	$S_{r+1} \ldots S_n$		
	F_1	$A_1 \ldots A_r$	$C_{r+1} \ldots C_n$		
Gambles	F_2	$B_1 \ldots B_r$	$C_{r+1} \ldots C_n$		
	G_1	$A_1 \ldots A_r$	$D_{r+1} \ldots D_n$		
	G_2	$B_1 \ldots B_r$	$D_{r+1} \ldots D_n$		

Provided possibilities are individuated as I have suggested, the STP may be supported by the following argument. A person may have reasons for preferring F_1 to F_2 and reasons for preferring F_2 to F_1. Whatever reasons she has, they must derive from what would be the case if S_1 were to occur, or from what would be the case if S_2 were to occur . . . or from what would be the case if S_n were to occur. More exactly, they must derive from the difference between $W(F_1, S_1)$ and $W(F_2, S_1)$, or from the difference between $W(F_1, S_2)$ and $W(F_2, S_2)$ . . . or from the difference between $W(F_1, S_n)$ and $W(F_2, S_n)$. But no reason can derive from the difference between $W(F_1, S_i)$ and $W(F_2, S_i)$ for any i between $r+1$ and n inclusive, because for these i $W(F_1, S_i)$ and $W(F_2, S_i)$ belong to the same possibility C_i and consequently do not differ in any justifier. So any reason there is for preferring F_1 to F_2 or F_2 to F_1 must derive from the difference between $W(F_1, S_i)$ and $W(F_2, S_i)$ for some i between 1 and r inclusive. Similarly any reason there is for preferring G_1 to G_2 or G_2 to G_1 must derive from the difference between $W(G_1, S_i)$ and $W(G_2, S_i)$ for some i between 1 and r inclusive. For any such i, $W(F_1, S_i)$ and $W(G_1, S_i)$ belong to the same possibility A_i, so they do not differ in any justifier. Likewise $W(F_2, S_i)$ and $W(G_2, S_i)$ do not differ in any justifier. Consequently, so far as justifiers are concerned any difference between $W(F_1, S_i)$ and $W(F_2, S_i)$ is also a difference between $W(G_1, S_i)$ and $W(G_2, S_i)$. So any reason there may be for preferring F_1 to F_2 or F_2 to F_1 is also a reason for preferring G_1 to G_2 or G_2 to G_1. If, therefore, a rational person prefers F_1 to F_2 she should also prefer G_1 to G_2.

This argument would work just as well if possibilities were more finely individuated than I have recommended, and differentiated by means of non-justifiers as well as justifiers. It will still be true that worlds classified under the same possibility do not differ in any justifier, which is all the argument requires. But under a finer individuation the STP will have less practical significance. It will be less of a constraint on practical preferences. Indeed, if we were to adopt the finest individuation, and classify each possible world as a different possibility, the STP would place no constraints at all on practical preferences. If the STP is going to constrain practical preferences there must at least be some practical preferences between gambles of the form shown in table 6.1. That is to say, there must be some gambles F_1, F_2, G_1 and G_2, of the form shown in table 6.1, such that it is possible for the person to have a choice between F_1 and F_2 and also possible for her to have a choice between G_1 and G_2. If the person were to have a choice between F_1 and F_2, and choose F_1, and if S_1 were to occur, then in the resulting world it would be true that:

(4) If S_n had occurred, C_n would have come about.

If, on the other hand, the person were to have a choice between G_1 and G_2, and choose G_1, and S_1 were to occur, this would not be true.[12] Table 6.1, however, shows that in either case the resulting possibility should be A_1. But, if possibilities are individuated to the finest degree, A_1 cannot include both a world where (4) is true and a world where it is false. Consequently the choice between F_1 and F_2 and the choice between G_1 and G_2 cannot both be possible.

Finer individuation, then, weakens the effectiveness of the STP. On the other hand, any coarser individuation than I have recommended invalidates the argument I have given, since it will allow a single possibility to include worlds that differ in a justifier. Coarser individuation will cause the STP to be false, as the examples I am coming to will show. My scheme of individuation gives the STP the greatest possible force consistent with its truth.

In arguments like the one I have given, the step most often criticised is the first, the claim that the reasons for preferring one gamble to another must derive from what would be the case if S_1 were to occur, or from what would be the case if S_2 were to occur, and so on. I compared the alternative gambles state by state. This state-by-state comparison is really the essence of the STP, and once it is granted the rest of the argument is not much more than a recital of the obvious. The objection to state-by-state comparison is that it seems

---

[12] Unless $D_n = C_n$. If $D_n = C_n$, use instead of n some i for which $D_i \neq C_i$.

to ignore any possible interaction there might be between states, between what would be the case if one state were to occur and what would be the case if another state were to occur.[13] But actually my way of individuating the possibilities makes sure that any interaction like this is taken account of in step-by-step comparison. The justification of step-by-step comparison, then, is simply that it takes account of everything there is to take account of. This is best explained by means of examples.

VII

I shall start with Allais' famous example, in Savage's version of it.[14] Let there be a hundred states of nature; say there is a fair lottery with a hundred tickets. Consider four possible gambles offering prizes according to table 6.2. Many people prefer f_1 to f_2 and g_2 to g_1, and Allais for one[15] has claimed that this pattern of preferences is rational. If it is, that seems to conflict with the STP because table 6.2 has the same pattern as table 6.1. According to Allais this is a case where state-by-state comparison of gambles is inadequate. There is a

Table 6.2

	States of nature (ticket numbers)		
	1	2–11	12–100
f_1	£1 million	£1 million	£1 million
Gambles f_2	0	£5 million	£1 million
g_1	£1 million	£1 million	0
g_2	0	£5 million	0

[13] This point about interaction, or 'complementarity' as it is often called, has been made by many people including Allais (1979), especially pp. 80–106, Manne (1952) and recently Loomes and Sugden (1984) and Sen (1985). The strongest reply to it is Samuelson's (1952), pp. 672–3. McLennan, in a very interesting article (1983), I think misses the point here. He says that to argue there is no complementarity 'serves only to remove one possible objection to the independence axiom'. But actually 'complementarity' is the name we give to interdependence between different goods, in this case between outcomes in different states of nature. If there is no complementarity there is no interdependence and the independence axiom is true.

[14] Allais (1979), p. 89, Savage (1972), p. 103.

[15] Eells (1982), pp. 39–40 for another.

reason for preferring f_1 to f_2 that is not derived either from what would be the case if ticket 1 came up, or from what would be the case if one of tickets 2–11 came up, or from what would be the case if one of tickets 12–100 came up. It is derived from all these together: taking them together it emerges that gamble f_1 gives a certainty of winning £1 million. Certainty, Allais believes, has a special value. This gives a reason for preferring f_1 to f_2 that is not also a reason for preferring g_1 to g_2.

Before this can be a complete rationalisation for preferring f_1 to f_2 and g_2 to g_1 we need to be told what the special value of certainty is. Why does the certainty of f_1 give a special reason for preferring it? The literature contains several more detailed rationalisations that answer this question,[16] and anyone who feels the appeal of these preferences can easily supply one for themselves. For instance, because the result of f_1 is certain, choosing f_1 may be a way to avoid anxiety; until the prize is announced any of the other gambles will keep you worrying that you may get nothing. Alternatively, picking the certainty of f_1 may be a way to avoid the chance of suffering bitter disappointment. If you picked f_2 instead, and got nothing, perhaps your extreme bad luck – losing a 99% chance of becoming rich – would make you very unhappy. By contrast, if you had a choice between g_1 and g_2, whichever you pick you are unlikely to win, so you will not be particularly disappointed if you lose. The common feature of all the rationalisations is that they depend on feelings. Besides the money prizes there are good and bad feelings of one sort or another to take into account. Let us write them into our table of results. If our rationalisation is the one I mentioned involving disappointment we shall get table 6.3. (Any other rationalisation would do equally well, and some are more plausible than this one; I choose it for its simplicity only.)

Now, is this feeling of disappointment enough to justify a preference or not? There has been some discussion of this question in the literature. Particularly at issue has been whether or not the feeling is irrational and, if it is, whether or not it is irrational to take it into account when forming a preference.[17] I have said enough about this in section V. It makes no difference to what I have to say now. Either the feeling is enough to justify a preference or it is not. If it is not, it would

---

[16] Bell (1982), p. 962, Eells (1982), pp. 39–40, Loomes and Sugden (1986).

[17] See Loomes and Sugden (1984), p. 10, Sen (1985), p. 117, Sugden (1985), pp. 174–5, Tversky (1975), pp. 171–2.

Table 6.3

	States of nature (ticket numbers)		
	1	2–11	12–100
f_1	£1 million	£1 million	£1 million
Gambles f_2	0; feel disappointed	£5 million	£1 million
g_1	£1 million	£1 million	0
g_2	0	£5 million	0

not be rational to prefer f_1 to f_2 and simultaneously g_2 to g_1. So the STP is not threatened. If it is, then, according to my scheme of individuation, getting nothing without disappointment must be reckoned a different possibility from getting nothing and feeling disappointed too. Table 6.3 therefore describes the possibilities more accurately than table 6.2. Table 6.3 does not have the pattern of table 6.1. So it is no violation of the STP to prefer f_1 to f_2 and g_2 to g_1. Again, the STP is not threatened.[18]

The very arguments, then, that aim to show why it is rational to prefer f_1 to f_2 and f_2 to g_1 also show, if they succeed, that these preferences do not violate the STP. They show that we must make distinctions between possibilities that were concealed by the original presentation of the example. The example seems to violate the STP only if one individuates by money prizes alone, ignoring feelings, and at the same time allows feelings to rationalise the preferences. But this creates a hopeless muddle. If disappointment, say, can make it rational to prefer f_1 to f_2 and g_2 to g_1, that is only because it is rational to prefer getting nothing without disappointment to getting nothing and feeling disappointed too. And if it is rational to prefer one thing to another they must obviously count as different possibilities.

Now we have an account of the Allais example we can see that state-by-state comparison handles it perfectly well. The reason there might be for preferring f_1 to f_2 – the reason that is not also a reason for preferring g_1 to g_2 – is that f_2 can lead to disappointment. And this reason derives simply from what would be the case if the first state occurs (ticket 1 comes up), since that is when the disappointment will happen. It is true that there is a sort of interaction between states, a causal one. If the first state occurs you feel disappointment because if any other state had occurred you would have become rich. Propriety does not allow us to say that your feeling is caused by what would otherwise have happened, since causes have to be actual events, but there is a causal connection. Nevertheless, this causal connection is not directly involved in forming a rational preference between f_1 and f_2. The reason there is for preferring f_1 is that under f_2 you feel disappointment in the first state, whatever its cause may be. If it had been caused differently it would still have been a reason. And it is a reason that will be picked up in the course of a state-by-state comparison.

Nearly all the published counterexamples[19] to the STP work in a similar way. They seem at first sight to contradict the STP because feelings are not taken into account when individuating the possibilities. The value of these examples is to demonstrate that, if feelings are justifiers, such a coarse individuation will cause the STP to fail. The right response is to individuate more finely, taking account of feelings. It is then entirely adequate to compare gambles state by state, as the STP assumes. Some authors have thought, however, that the examples should lead us to abandon the STP itself. Several of them have had a considered reason for being suspicious of fine individuation. I shall come to this in section IX.

VIII

Before that, however, I must mention one example that raises more interesting questions. It was invented by Peter Diamond.[20] Suppose some good can be given to either of two people but not both, say a sweet to one child out of two, or a kidney transplant to one patient out of two. Suppose there are two states of nature, say a coin's landing heads or tails. Consider the gambles in table 6.4. Diamond believes it would in certain circumstances be rational for a person (not one of the two subjects) to prefer ϕ_1 to ϕ_2 and γ_2 to γ_1. Since table 6.4 has the pattern of table 6.1 this seems to contradict the STP. Of

[19] For instance Drèze (1974), p. 15, perhaps Machina (1981), p. 172 but see Note 26, and Sen's first two examples (1985), pp. 118–20. Ellsberg's examples (1961, pp. 650–6) have been treated similarly – by appealing to feelings – by Bell (1985) and Eells (1982, p. 39). But I have to say that I find this treatment less plausible for these examples. Ellsberg's examples, unlike the others, are aimed against the personalist theory of probability, and that is a subject I would rather not broach here.

[20] Diamond (1967).

Table 6.4

	States of nature	(results of toss)
	Heads	Tails
ϕ_1	Neil gets good	Maggie gets good
Gambles ϕ_2	Maggie gets good	Maggie gets good
γ_1	Neil gets good	Neil gets good
γ_2	Maggie gets good	Neil gets good

course, these preferences are not self-interested, but even non-self-interested preferences should be coherent. (If you believe that rationality requires self-interest this section is not addressed to you.)

To purify the example, let us assume that the people's feelings depend only on who gets the good. For instance, if ϕ_1 were chosen and heads came up the people's feelings would be exactly the same as they would be if γ_1 were chosen and heads came up. We might assume, for instance, that the process of selecting who is to get the good is kept secret from the candidates. So feelings give no grounds for a finer discrimination between possibilities than is shown in table 6.4.

In ϕ_1 and γ_2 the selection of who is to get the good is made randomly, and in ϕ_2 and γ_1 it is not. Diamond believes that in some circumstances fairness requires a random selection. It is in those circumstances that he thinks it would be rational to prefer ϕ_1 to ϕ_2 and γ_2 to γ_1.

Suppose, then, the circumstances are such that fairness requires random selection. Then if ϕ_1 is chosen and heads comes up it will be the case that the process of selection is fair. But if γ_1 is chosen and heads comes up this will not be the case. And so on. Table 6.5 incorporates these facts. Suppose now that the fairness of selection is a justifier; it is rational to prefer a possibility where selection is fair to one where it is not. Then we must classify a world where selection is fair in a different possibility from a world where selection is not fair. Table 6.5 therefore represents the possibilities more accurately than table 6.4. Since table 6.5 does not have the pattern of table 6.1, preferring ϕ_1 to ϕ_2 and γ_2 to γ_1 no longer seems to violate the STP.

But is the fairness of selection a justifier? If it is, it is one that does not depend on feelings. I have assumed away differences of feelings. The utilitarian tradition, as I said in section V, suggests that only

Table 6.5

		States of nature	(results of toss)
		Heads	Tails
Gambles	ϕ_1	Neil gets good Selection fair	Maggie gets good Selection fair
	ϕ_2	Maggie gets good Selection not fair	Maggie gets good Selection not fair
	γ_1	Neil gets good Selection not fair	Neil gets good Selection not fair
	γ_2	Maggie gets good Selection fair	Neil gets good Selection fair

differences of feelings can be justifiers. Part of the value of this example, I think, is that it provides a plausible counterexample to that view.[21] But if fairness is not a justifier then the example poses no threat to the STP in the first place; once differences of feelings have been excluded nothing can make it rational to prefer ϕ_1 to ϕ_2 and γ_2 to γ_1.[22]

My way of rescuing the STP from Diamond's example may well look too facile. It treats fairness of selection as a feature of the world that results from a particular choice of gamble in a particular state of nature. But the point of the example seems to be that fairness is not a feature of what happens in one state. It is a feature of what happens in the two states taken together: that Neil gets the good in one state and Maggie in the other. Fairness is not identifiable within a single state, so that state-by-state comparison seems inadequate. It is true (in appropriate circumstances) that the selection is fair in $W(\phi_1, \text{heads})$, the world that results if ϕ_1 is chosen in preference to ϕ_2 and heads comes up (so Neil gets the good). But what makes it true is that if tails had come up Maggie would have got the good. I have classified $W(\phi_1, \text{heads})$ and $W(\gamma_1, \text{heads})$ into different possibilities because the selection is fair in one and not in the other. But the only thing that makes this difference is what would have happened if the coin had landed tails. The difference depends, then, not on what happens in the

[21] See Broome (1984a, b).
[22] This is, for instance, the view of Deschamps and Gevers (1979).

state of nature we are talking about, but on what happens in the other. In order to decide what possibility occurs in one state we need to know what would have happened in the other state. This is why Diamond's example is much more effective than the others. In the others the interaction between states is merely causal, and to decide what possibility occurs in one state we need only know what happens in that state (including feelings). Here the interaction is logical.

Nevertheless, the fact is that the proposition:

(5)   The selection is fair

is (given the conditions that make random selection fair) one of the things that are the case in $W(\phi_1, \text{heads})$, and it is not one of the things that are the case in $W(\gamma_1, \text{heads})$. Since I am taking this proposition to be a justifier, $W(\phi_1, \text{heads})$ and $W(\gamma_1, \text{heads})$ must be classified as different possibilities. Proposition (5) is not any the less true in $W(\phi_1, \text{heads})$ because part of what makes it true is the truth of the counterfactual conditional proposition

(6)   If the coin had landed tails Maggie would have got the good.

Proposition (6) is, one might say, *about* a different world, but it is certainly true in $W(\phi_1, \text{heads})$, and so is (5). This sort of thing is common: many ordinary propositions that are true in one world are made true by counterfactual conditions that are about another world. For instance, 'Charles I's crown was soluble in *aqua regia*', which is true in our actual world, is equivalent to 'If Charles I's crown had been placed in *aqua regia* it would have dissolved'. But actually it was never placed in *aqua regia*; it was melted down in Cromwell's time.[23]

---

[23] The predicates 'lucky' and 'unlucky' are a bit like 'soluble'. A person is unlucky, roughly speaking, if and only if, had things gone differently, she would have been better off than she actually is. The point of Machina's interesting example (1981, p. 172) is that congratulatory behaviour is appropriate towards a lucky person and sympathetic behaviour towards an unlucky one. The example can be treated as I have treated Diamond's. The justifier here is 'I behave appropriately'. Given that, say, I behave sympathetically, this justifier is true if and only if the person is unlucky, which is true if and only if, had things gone differently, she would have been better off. So as in Diamond's example the justifier is made true by a counter-factual conditional. But I find Machina's example slightly less convincing than Diamond's. I suspect that the appropriateness of sympathetic behaviour is not determined by whether or not the recipient is actually unlucky, but by whether or not she feels unlucky, or perhaps by whether or not she believes she is unlucky. If this is so, 'I behave appropriately' is made true, not by a counterfactual conditional but by an unconditional proposition about the person's actual beliefs or feelings. This puts the

There is, then, nothing wrong with my treatment of Diamond's example, however facile it may seem. And the arguments of sections III–V require that the example be treated this way. If a proposition that is a justifier is true in one of two worlds and false in the other, the worlds must be classed as different possibilities. In the example the justifier is that the selection is fair. Its truth depends on a counterfactual conditional that is about another world. But there is nothing wrong with that.

IX

Most critics of the STP would, I think, agree that a defence like the one I have mounted is perfectly possible. They recognise that a fine enough individuation of possibilities will save the STP from the counterexamples. But they believe that this sort of defence achieves a hollow victory. It drains the STP of its significance and leaves it empty.[24] I have already said what truth there is in this idea. The more finely possibilities are individuated the less do the axioms of coherence – transitivity as well as the STP – constrain practical preferences. If the individuation is the very finest, they do not constrain practical preferences at all. And there is surely something

example in the same class as Allais'. Of course, King Charles's crown had an ordinary property, determinable without reference outside the actual world, that caused it to be soluble in *aqua regia*: the property of being gold. But 'Charles I's crown was soluble in *aqua regia*' is not logically equivalent to 'Charles I's crown was made of gold'. Likewise, if the selection between Neil and Maggie is fair there is presumably a condition determinable without reference outside the actual world that causes this to be so. Perhaps the condition is this: whoever is distributing the good intends to let the result of the coin-toss determine who gets it. This intention is straightforwardly something that exists in the actual world, and it is this that causes the selection to be fair. It might conceivably be argued that the connection is not merely causal but logical: the selection is fair if and only if the person distributing the good has this intention. If this were true then 'The selection is fair' would be made true, not by a counterfactual conditional, but by an unconditional proposition about the person's intentions in the actual world. Diamond's example would be reduced to the same class as Allais'. But actually I think this is wrong. It is not the intention that makes the selection fair (except causally) but the fact that the other person would have got the good if the toss had gone differently. If the person distributing the good had had the intention but for some reason it would not have been carried out if the toss had gone differently, then I do not think the selection was fair.

24   The danger of making the theory empty is mentioned by MacCrimmon and Larsson (1979), p. 398, Machina (1981), p. 173, Samuelson (1966), p. 136 and Tversky (1975), p. 171.

wrong with this. Coherence, surely, must impose some practical limits on our preferences.

The remedy is to stop short of the finest individuation. We must, of course, have *some* scheme of individuation. Critics of the STP have implicitly adopted arbitrary and coarse schemes. For instance, they have individuated by money prizes,[25] or by 'physically observable aspects',[26] or by 'everything in the real world (except in [the] mind)'.[27] Such schemes have generally been taken for granted by both sides in the discussion. The supporters of the STP seem to have wanted to defend it even when individuating by money prizes only.[28] The critics are right to point out how implausible the STP is in these conditions.[29] But in principle the need for a finer individuation has always been recognised.[30] And what we need is not an arbitrary scheme but one that is founded on good arguments. A line must be drawn somewhere between propositions that will be used to individuate possibilities and those that will not. Merely to point out the danger of too fine an individuation – that it will make the STP empty – is not enough to determine where to draw the line.

I believe my scheme draws it in precisely the right place: between propositions that justify a preference and those that do not. Remember that I drew the line here because it gives the axiom of transitivity just the right force. Any finer individuation and the axiom would be too weak; any coarser and we should have the nonsense of a rational preference between a possibility and itself. Only later did it turn out that the same scheme gives the STP just the right force too. It is coherence as a whole, not merely the STP, that is at stake here.

Drawing the boundary between justifiers and non-justifiers amounts to setting up some principles of rationality: rationality requires a person to be indifferent between classes of worlds that differ only in non-justifiers. These principles of indifference are logically prior to the principles of coherence because they determine precisely what the principles of coherence mean. I imagine that some critics of the STP may be sceptical about the existence of these principles of indifference. They may believe that rationality requires coherence only. But, as I said in section IV, the penalty attached to

[25] For instance, Allais in the example discussed in section VII – but this is very common.   [26] Machina (1981), p. 173.   [27] Sen (1985), p. 121.

[28] See, for instance, Savage's response to Allais' example (Savage 1972), p. 103.

[29] This point has been impressed on me by Ole Hagen and Robert Sugden.

[30] See Drèze (1974), p. 8, who quotes Savage (1972), p. 25, and Arrow (1970), p. 45: 'In the description of a consequence is included all that the agent values'.

this view is that rationality will not then constrain practical preferences at all. The critics are right to say that, without principles of indifference, the STP will have no practical force. Nor will transitivity. I shall not argue with anyone who is willing to pay this penalty. But I do not believe that many critics of the STP will be so nihilistic about rationality. Most, I think, will at least agree that propositions like (1) and (4) are not, by themselves, enough to justify a preference. If so, they will have to agree that a line must be drawn somewhere between justifiers and non-justifiers.[31]

Suppose somebody has preferences that seem to conflict with the STP, and claims they are rational. What I am saying amounts simply to this: her claim will need justifying. The justification will consist in pointing out a difference, sufficient to justify a preference, between possibilities that seemed at first to be the same. It is a tribute to the STP that when its critics have presented counterexamples – preferences they claim to be rational and that seem to breach the STP – they have generally felt the need to justify them in this way. In making such a justification necessary the STP shows it is not empty but has substantive content. Either the justification will succeed or it will fail. If it fails the STP is unscathed. If it succeeds it will show that the preferences seemed to conflict with the STP only because possibilities were individuated too coarsely. Possibilities that seemed to be the same are in fact different. The preferences will turn out not to conflict with the STP at all.

Whether or not a justification succeeds depends on which propositions are justifiers and which are not. To settle that, one needs a substantive theory of rationality. On this I have avoided taking sides, though I mentioned some alternative views in section V. I have said only that the theory cannot simply be: any proposition is a justifier. I do not expect much opposition to this, at least from economists. The commonest view I find amongst economists is that only feelings are justifiers.

X

There is another way in which the victory won by my defence of the STP could turn out to be a hollow one. The STP's purpose is to stand

---

[31] Tversky (1975, pp. 171–2) presents an argument that is, if I understand it, close to mine. And his conclusion is the same as mine: 'I believe that an adequate analysis of rational choice cannot accept the evaluation of consequences as given, and examine only the consistency of preferences.'

as one of the foundations of the expected utility theory of rationality. This theory says that a rational person's preferences can be represented by expected utility; it will be possible to define utilities and probabilities for the person in such a way that she prefers one gamble to another if and only if the former has the higher expected utility. Furthermore, the probabilities will be unique, and the utilities will be unique up to linear transformations. Expected utility theory can be derived from a set of axioms including the STP. If I have defended the STP in a way that puts one of the other axioms in doubt, that would indeed look like a hollow victory. Expected utility theory would still have no solid foundation.

And actually my defence of the STP does put one of the other axioms in doubt. It is Savage's first axiom,[32] and it says that there is a complete preference ordering among gambles. A gamble can be thought of as a function from states of nature to possibilities. To each state the function assigns a possibility, the possibility that will result if the gamble is chosen and the state occurs. Savage's first axiom assumes that *any* function from states to possibilities is a gamble that has a place in the preference ordering. That is to say, any arbitrary gamble can always be constructed out of possibilities, and it will have a place in the preference ordering. In particular, corresponding to every possibility there is in the preference ordering a 'constant gamble', a gamble that is certain to result in that possibility whatever state of nature may occur.

Look back at my account of Allais' example. In one of the possibilities I mentioned you get no money and also suffer disappointment. The cause of your disappointment is your bad luck; in any other state you would have won a fortune. Is there a constant gamble that results in this possibility whatever the state of nature? Such a constant gamble is probably causally impossible, because you can probably only feel precisely this sort of disappointment in one state if you would have won a fortune in the other states. And look at my account of Diamond's example. In one of the possibilities I mentioned Neil gets the good and the selection is fair. Is there a constant gamble that results in this possibility in either state of nature? If the conditions are such that fairness can only be achieved by random selection, then in a constant gamble where Neil gets the good in either state the selection cannot possibly be fair. Here the impossibility is logical rather than causal. Savage's axiom assumes that impossible

---

[32] Savage (1972), p. 18.

gambles like these have a place in a person's preference ordering. And this is not very plausible. Certainly, of course, they can have no place in a person's practical preferences.[33]

This is a problem. In fact I think this is the real problem that is raised by the objections to the STP, rather than any difficulty with the STP itself. It is the result, of course, of the fine individuation I have recommended. The first point I want to make about it is that it is not such a serious problem for expected utility theory as difficulties with the STP would be. If expected utility theory is true the STP follows as a consequence. So if the STP is false the theory is false. But if Savage's first axiom is false the theory may very well be true all the same.

The second point I want to make is that this first axiom has never seemed plausible from the start, for reasons that have nothing to do with the new problem I have raised.[34] Consequently there are already in existence several theories that derive expected utility theory without it, using weaker axioms instead.[35] So far as I know, none of them completely solves our new problem,[36] but they give good reason to hope it is soluble.

[33] A rough way of putting the point made in this paragraph is that the nature of a possibility may depend on the probability of its occurrence. I have to thank Angus Deaton for pointing out this difficulty to me.

[34] See, for instance, Eells (1982), pp. 83–4, Fishburn (1981), pp. 162–3, Jeffrey (1983), pp. 156–62.   [35] See the comprehensive survey in Fishburn (1981).

[36] There is, for instance, Fishburn's theory, where preferences are defined on 'act-event pairs' (1982), chapter 12. This theory fails to solve the problem completely because Fishburn assumes the existence of 'mixed acts'. If f is the act of giving the good to Neil and g the act of giving it to Maggie, there is the mixed act that is 'implemented by flipping a fair coin and using f if "heads" and g if "tails"' (Fishburn 1974), p. 33. This mixed act is assumed to lie in the preference order between f and g. But we have learned from Diamond that this may not be so.

The problem, basically, is to make sure that the given preferences are rich enough to determine probabilities uniquely, and utilities up to a linear transformation. An alternative approach to this problem is to build more structure into the theory so that it needs fewer data to work on. This approach is exemplified by the work of Loomes and Sugden (1982, 1986). They make specific assumptions about what determines people's feelings. Where it is feelings that are causing the problem, as it is in Allais' example, this is enough to let them determine probabilities and utilities (1982, Appendix). This approach is obviously not general enough to be a complete solution.

Peter Hammond's interesting new proof of expected utility theory (1988) is based on very weak assumptions. The STP, indeed, is proved by Hammond rather than assumed. He individuates possibilities finely enough to allow this. His approach, however, does not solve our problem either. He makes an assumption of unrestricted domain, which has much the effect of Savage's first axiom. With fine individuation it is equally unacceptable (see Hammond's note 4, p. 77).

I myself favour Richard Jeffrey's theory.[37] Jeffrey does not assign utilities to possibilities, which are combined by forming gambles, but to propositions, which are combined by forming truth-functions. His theory does not depend on gambles in any way, so it does not require impossible gambles to have a place in the preference order. And truth-functional combination does not seem to be attended by the same difficulty. Jeffrey regards this as his theory's chief virtue.[38]

Savage uses arbitrary gambles for three purposes. One is to obtain an ordering of events by probability,[39] and another is to scale utilities.[40] Jeffrey does these jobs by other means.[41] The third purpose is to derive preferences between possibilities from preferences between gambles. It is preferences between gambles that Savage takes as given, and one possibility he takes to be preferred to another if and only if the constant gamble corresponding to the first is preferred to the constant gamble corresponding to the second.[42] For this he obviously requires that every possibility has a corresponding constant gamble somewhere in the preference ordering. This third job Jeffrey frankly does not do at all. He simply takes as given to him preferences amongst all the propositions he has to deal with. For instance, the proposition:

(7)   Neil gets the good and the selection is fair

he assumes to have a given place in the preference ordering. Savage would want to deduce the place of this proposition from the place of the corresponding constant gamble in the preference ordering of gambles. The difficulty we found with that project is that the corresponding constant gamble is impossible. Jeffrey has not solved this difficulty but skirted round it.

Is this an important failing in Jeffrey's theory? Why, anyway, did Savage want to start from preferences between gambles? The reason is that he wanted to start from preferences that could in principle be revealed by choice, from practical preferences, that is to say.[43] He believed, his remarks clearly imply, that practical preferences are epistemologically a more secure foundation than non-practical ones. Jeffrey, on the other hand, is happy to take non-practical preferences for granted. For instance, he would take for granted a preference

---

[37] Jeffrey (1983).   [38] *Ibid.*, p. 157.   [39] Savage (1972), pp. 30–3.
[40] *Ibid.*, pp. 73–6.   [41] Jeffrey (1983), chapters 7 and 8.
[42] Savage (1972), p. 25.   [43] *Ibid.*, p. 17.

between proposition (7) and some other proposition, even though (7) could never be chosen. (If you choose that Neil gets the good, his selection cannot be fair, since I am assuming that only a random selection would be fair.)

I, like Jeffrey, am willing to accept some non-practical preferences as given.[44] Against Savage's attitude I have three things to say. First, I am not sure why he thinks practical preferences are particularly secure epistemologically, and this needs to be explained. Second, it was hopeless from the start to try and found the theory on what could in principle be revealed by choices. Savage requires that some pairs of gambles are indifferent to each other, and as he himself points out, choices cannot distinguish preference from indifference.[45] Third, what we are concerned with, and Savage too,[46] is a theory of rationality, not of actual choices. As I have said, it would be a poor theory of rationality that did not say *anything* about practical preferences, that did not constrain them in any way. But I cannot see why a theory of rationality should be concerned with practical preferences exclusively, and I cannot see why the epistemological status of preferences should be relevant at all to a theory of rationality.

The STP, being a condition on gambles, is not an axiom of Jeffrey's theory. But, since it is a consequence of any expected utility theory, his theory requires it to be true. If there happen to be gambles of the form shown in table 6.1, and F_1 is preferred to F_2, then G_1 must be preferred to G_2. The theory would treat the counterexamples in the way I have treated them. This treatment is natural to Jeffrey's system. In evaluating the outcome of a gamble in a particular state of nature, Jeffrey would naturally take account of every proposition that would then be true. This would include propositions describing the state of people's feelings, and also the proposition that the particular gamble had been chosen and the proposition that the particular state of nature had occurred.[47] In effect, Jeffrey allows any proposition to distinguish one possibility from another. He adopts, in fact, the very finest individuation of possibilities. I have been using a coarser scheme than this, but I mentioned in section IV that it would in many ways be better to use the finest individuation and supplement it with

---

[44] So too is Fishburn. One of his theories (Fishburn 1982, chapter 12) takes as given preferences between 'act-event pairs', and these are non-practical.
[45] Savage (1972), p. 17.   [46] Savage (1972), p. 7.
[47] See Eells (1982), pp. 79–80.

explicit principles of rational indifference. These principles are needed, I explained, to make sure that the requirements of coherence place some restrictions on practical preferences. Since Jeffrey does not distinguish practical from non-practical preferences, the need for these principles escapes him. In a more complete theory of rationality they would have to be added to his axioms of coherence.

XI

I believe that the sure-thing principle is sound, and that the objections that have been made to it give us no reason to doubt the expected utility theory of rationality.

References

Allais, M. (1979), 'The Foundations of a Positive Theory of Choice Involving Risk and a Criticism of the Postulates and Axioms of the American School', in M. Allais and O. Hagen (eds.) (1979), 27–145.

Allais, M. and Hagen, O. (eds.) (1979), *Expected Utility Hypothesis and the Allais Paradox*, Dordrecht: Reidel.

Arrow, K.J. (1970), *Essays in the Theory of Risk-Bearing*, Amsterdam: North-Holland.

Bell, D.E. (1982), 'Regret in Decision Making Under Uncertainty', *Operations Research*, 30: 961–81.

(1985), 'Disappointment in Decision Making Under Uncertainty', *Operations Research*, 33: 1–27.

Broome, J. (1984a), 'Selecting People Randomly', *Ethics*, 95: 38–55.

(1984b), 'Uncertainty and Fairness', *Economic Journal*, 94: 624–32.

(1991), *Weighing Goods*, Oxford: Basil Blackwell.

Deschamps, R. and Gevers, L. (1979), 'Separability, Risk-Bearing and Social Welfare Judgements', in J. Laffont (ed.), *Aggregation and Revelation of Preferences*, Amsterdam: North Holland, 145–60.

Diamond, P.A. (1967), 'Cardinal Welfare, Individualistic Ethics, and Interpersonal Comparisons of Utility: Comment', *Journal of Political Economy*, 75: 765–6.

Drèze, J.H. (1974), 'Axiomatic Theories of Choice, Cardinal Utility and Subjective Probability: A Review', in J.H. Drèze (ed.), *Allocation Under Uncertainty: Equilibrium and Optimality*, London: Macmillan.

Eells, E. (1982), *Rational Decision and Causality*, Cambridge University Press.

Ellsberg, D. (1961), 'Risk, Ambiguity and the Savage Axioms', *Quarterly Journal of Economics*, 75: 643–69.

Fishburn, P.C. (1974), 'On the Foundations of Decision Making Under Uncertainty', in M. Balch, D. McFadden and S. Wu (eds.), *Essays on*

Economic Behavior Under Uncertainty, Amsterdam: North Holland, 25–44.

(1981), 'Subjective Expected Utility: A Review of Normative Theories', *Theory and Decision*, 13: 139–99.

(1982), *The Foundations of Expected Utility*, Dordrecht: Reidel.

Griffin, J. (1986), *Well-Being: Its Meaning, Measurement and Moral Importance*, Oxford University Press.

Hammond, P.J. (1988), 'Consequential Foundations for Expected Utility', *Theory and Decision*, 25; 25–78.

Hurley, S. (1985), 'Supervenience and the Possibility of Coherence', *Mind*, 94: 501–25.

Jeffrey, R.C. (1983), *The Logic of Decision*, Second Edition, University of Chicago Press.

Loomes, G. and Sugden, R. (1982). 'Regret Theory: An Alternative Theory of Rational Choice Under Uncertainty', *Economic Journal*, 42: 805–24.

(1984), 'The Importance of What Might Have Been', in O. Hagen and F. Wenstøp (eds.) (1984), *Progress in Utility and Risk Theory*, Dordrecht: Reidel.

(1986), 'Disappointment and Dynamic Consistency in Choice Under Uncertainty', *Review of Economic Studies*, 53: 271–82.

MacCrimmon, K.R. and Larsson, S. (1979), 'Utility Theory: Axioms Versus "Paradoxes"', in M. Allais and O. Hagen (eds.) (1979), pp. 333–409.

Machina, M.J. (1981), '"Rational" Decision Making Versus "Rational" Decision Modelling?', *Journal of Mathematical Psychology*, 24: 163–75.

Manne, A.S. (1952), 'The Strong Independence Assumption – Gasoline Blends and Probability Mixtures', *Econometrica*, 20: 665–8.

McLennan, E.F. (1983), 'Sure-Thing Doubts', in B.P. Stigum and F. Wenstøp (eds.), *Foundations of Utility and Risk Theory with Applications*, Dordrecht: Reidel, 117–36.

Parfit, D. (1984), *Reasons and Persons*, Oxford University Press.

Samuelson, P.A. (1952), 'Probability, Utility and the Independence Axiom', *Econometrica*, 20: 670–8.

(1966), 'Utility, Preference, and Probability', in J.E. Stiglitz (ed.), *The Collected Scientific Papers of Paul A. Samuelson*, MIT Press, 127–36.

Savage, L.J. (1972), *The Foundations of Statistics*, Second Edition, Dover.

Sen, A. (1985), 'Rationality and Uncertainty', *Theory and Decision*, 18: 109–27.

Sugden, R. (1985), 'Why Be Consistent? A Critical Analysis of Consistency Requirements in Choice Theory', *Economica*, 52: 167–83.

Tversky, A. (1967), 'Additivity, Utility and Subjective Probability', *Journal of Mathematical Psychology*, 4: 175–201.

(1975), 'A Critique of Expected Utility Theory: Descriptive and Normative Considerations', *Erkenntis*, 9: 163–73.

7   Animal spirits*

ROBIN MATTHEWS

I

Let me begin by reading three well-known passages from chapter 12 of Keynes's *General Theory*, the chapter on 'The Long Run State of Expectation':

it is probable that the actual average results of investments . . . have disappointed the hopes that prompted them . . . If human nature felt no temptation to take a chance, no satisfaction (profit apart) in constructing a factory, a railway, a mine, or a farm, there might not be much investment merely as a result of cold calculation. (p. 150)

Most, probably, of our decisions to do something positive, the full consequences of which will be drawn out over many days to come, can only be taken as a result of animal spirits – of a spontaneous urge to action rather than inaction, and not as the outcome of a weighted average of quantitative benefits multiplied by quantitative probabilities. Enterprise only pretends to itself to be actuated by the statements in its own prospectus. (pp. 161–2)

. . . human decisions affecting the future, whether personal or political or economic, cannot depend on strict mathematical expectation, since the basis for making such calculations does not exist . . . it is our innate urge to activity that makes the wheels go round . . . (pp. 162–3)

Thus animal spirits are conceived by Keynes as a feature of human nature that serves to give a pervasive, positive impulse to investment.

* A revised version of the Keynes Lecture, delivered to the British Academy on 7 June 1984. I am greatly indebted, for helpful information, suggestions, and comments, to Moses Abramovitz, Kenneth Arrow, Margaret Bray, Stephen Dunnett, Frank Hahn, Richard Kahn, Gay Meeks, Don Moggridge, Tad Rybczynski, Tibor Scitovsky, Amartya Sen, and Aubrey Silberston. Responsibility for remaining errors is entirely my own.

We are grateful to the British Academy for permission to reprint this paper from the *Proceedings of the British Academy*, London, vol. 70 (1984), pp. 209–29, Oxford University Press.

It is a feature intimately related to uncertainty. The reason for this is that animal spirits manifest themselves largely in the way that people respond to uncertainty:

Individual initiative will only be adequate when reasonable calculation is supplemented and supported by animal spirits, so that the thought of ultimate loss . . . is put aside as a healthy man puts aside the expectation of death.   (p. 162)

The passage about the satisfaction of building a railway could be taken to mean that the activity of investment carries with it a non-pecuniary utility, in principle quite independent of uncertainty. That may be part of what Keynes had in mind, but no more than part. He clearly regarded the connection with uncertainty as being of the essence.

Uncertainty is the main theme of chapter 12. Keynes there draws on his *Treatise on Probability* to reject the frequency theory of probability as applied to uncertainty (in the sense of Frank Knight). The associated concept of animal spirits takes second place in chapter 12 to a separate associated question, the volatility of investment – and, incidentally, animal spirits are not mentioned in the article in *QJE*, 1937, in which Keynes developed his treatment of uncertainty further. The volatility arises partly because the bases of expectations about the future of the real economy are so insecure that those expectations are subject to violent changes. It also arises partly because of Stock Exchange fluctuations. Those have a different source, namely the instability of a purely speculative market where everyone's chief preoccupation is to outguess everyone else. As Richard Kahn has pointed out,[1] the discussion in chapter 12 shifts about rather confusingly between decisions about real capital formation and decisions about operations on the Stock Exchange. There are some inconsistencies in it about whether Stock Exchange fluctuations have important effects on real investment or not.[2] These inconsistencies are not relevant to what I have to say here. But it is relevant, and introduces a further point, to note the words Keynes uses to indicate how equity prices may affect investment:

[1] Kahn (1984).
[2] Chapter 12 was apparently written less carefully and in a more light-hearted spirit than most of the *General Theory*. It was not subjected to the scrutiny of the group of younger colleagues assembled by Keynes to help him (information from Richard Kahn).

. . . there is no sense in building up a new enterprise at a cost greater than that at which a similar existing enterprise may be purchased . . .
[likewise]
there is an inducement to spend on a new project what may seem to be an exorbitant sum if it can be floated off on the Stock Exchange at an immediate profit. (p. 151)

This passage follows immediately after the first of the quotations that I cited about animal spirits. It's introduced as a complication that applies in a world of quoted joint stock companies as opposed to a world of owner-managers. The suggestion is evidently that there are limits to the influences of animal spirits; people are not so inebriated by them that they prefer course *A* to course *B* if course *B* *certainly* brings a greater profit.

The hypothesis, then, is that people – or at least some people – are predisposed towards action rather than inaction and hence are predisposed to ignore some of the downside risks of action; that this serves as a stimulus to investment to an extent that is positive on average; but that it does not override unambiguous prospects of gain or loss. The hypothesis is thus a reasonably specific one; it certainly doesn't imply, as it's sometimes been supposed to do, that the determination of investment is entirely arbitrary.[3]

What I should like to do is to try to relate this type of idea to some more recent thinking about the psychology of economic behaviour, and then to revert to appraise its significance for investment and also for other aspects of economic life.

This is not intended as a lecture on the history of thought, but a few words first on antecedents will be useful to broaden the idea somewhat.

I asked Don Moggridge if he knew the origins of the phrase 'animal spirits' in Keynes's own thinking. He has very kindly sent me the following interesting information.

The origins of 'animal spirits' seem to go a long way back in Keynes. The earliest reference comes in a set of lecture notes, which are in the Marshall Library collection, entitled 'Notes on Modern Philosophy I – Descartes,

---

[3] The hypothesis was made more specific still in later work by Joan Robinson. 'For purposes of our model, therefore, the "animal spirits" of the firms can be expressed in terms of a function relating the desired rate of growth of the stock of productive capital to the expected level of profits' (1962, p. 38). This definition does not bring in uncertainty, but Mrs Robinson no doubt regarded the role of uncertainty in investment decisions as so pervasive as not to need to be explicitly underlined.

Leibnitz, McTaggart's Lectures, Ertemann's History – [includes Spinoza's Ethics]'. In the part concerning Descartes as regards life and biology the text runs 'The body is moved by animal spirits – the fiery particles of the blood distilled by the heat of the heart. They move the body by penetrating and moving the nerves and muscles . . . But does not this increase the amount of motion? No, for the animal spirits are always in motion – the will only directs them.'

Keynes then adds a comment that reads 'unconscious mental action'.

I don't know what was the process by which this youthful reflection matured in Keynes's mind. It's noteworthy that animal spirits is a phrase that was also used by the philosopher Hume, so greatly admired by Keynes.[4]

Be that as it may, it had been characteristic of the Cambridge school of economics since Marshall to give a significant amount of attention to the psychological springs of economic behaviour; admittedly, they were never placed in the forefront, nor were they very satisfactorily accommodated in the main body of doctrine. We have the well-known invocation by Pigou of waves of optimism and pessimism in the explanation of the cycle, an idea which builds on a passage by Marshall (*Principles*, p. 711) attributing the persistence of recessions to lack of confidence. There is a good passage, in a similar sense, in a book by another Cambridge economist of that time, F. Lavington's *The Trade Cycle* (1922). Lavington illustrates the epidemic quality of business confidence by a comparison with skaters who judge the safety of the ice on the pond by the number of people already upon it (pp. 31–7). He points out interestingly that, although this *may* lead to disaster, it is in itself not wholly unreasonable – there is some sense, in face of uncertainty, if a person supplements his own judgement by the judgements formed by other people; for all he knows, they may have access to information that he lacks.

These ideas from Pigou and Lavington concern uncertainty generally and its relation to fluctuations, rather than animal spirits.

---

[4] Hume (1739), *A Treatise on Human Nature*, Book 1, Part iv, Section vii. I am grateful to Gay Meeks for pointing this out to me. See her essay in this volume. Don Moggridge suggests to me that Keynes's continuing interest in Hume and Descartes in the 1930s was connected with his activities as a book-collector. He was buying Descartes's writings in 1934, the year when chapter 12 was substantially written, and his interest in Hume was stimulated by his acquisition of a copy of the very rare *An Abstract of a Book Lately Published; Entitled a Treatise of Human Nature . . .*, attributed by Keynes and Sraffa to Hume himself. *Collected Works of John Maynard Keynes*, vol. 13 (1973), p. 423; ibid., vol. 27 (1980), pp. 373–90; Munby in Milo Keynes (ed.) (1975), pp. 292–3; Exhibition Catalogue of the Fitzwilliam Museum (1983), p. 66.

But going a little further back in the Cambridge canon, that notion is also present. The combination of uncertainty and animal spirits could hardly be expressed more clearly than it is by the conjunction of the two quotations which Dennis Robertson used to preface his 1915 *Study of Industrial Fluctuation*. The first is from Heraclitus: πάντα ῥεῖ ('everything is in flux'): uncertainty. The second is from Walt Whitman: 'Urge and urge and urge, always the procreant urge of the world': animal spirits. A little later, some similar ideas, applied to the theory of consumption, were put forward by R.G. Hawtrey, another associate of Keynes, in *The Economic Problem* (1926). Perhaps most interesting of all is the chapter from the fountain head itself, Marshall's *Principles*, entitled 'Wants in Relation to Activities' (pp. 86–91). Marshall refers there to the desire for variety for its own sake and the desire for distinction, and then goes on to say 'The desire for excellence [in performance] for its own sake, is almost as wide in its range as the lower desire for distinction'. He concludes as follows:

It is not true therefore that 'the Theory of Consumption is the scientific basis of economics'. For much that is of chief interest in the science of wants, is borrowed from the science of efforts and activities. These two supplement one another; either is incomplete without the other. But if either, more than the other, may claim to be the interpreter of the history of man, whether on the economic side or any other, it is the science of activities and not that of wants; and McCulloch indicated their true relations when, discussing 'the progressive nature of man', he said – 'The gratification of a want or a desire is merely a step to some new pursuit. In every stage of his progress he is destined to contrive and invent, to engage in new undertakings; and when these are accomplished to enter with fresh energy upon others'.

Potentially, as I shall argue, these are ideas with some radical and far-reaching implications for economics. Activity itself – travelling hopefully – assumes as much importance as a motive for economic behaviour as the consequence of action – arriving. However, Marshall didn't follow up the suggestion – nor, to tell the truth, is it very clearly spelt out in the chapter I've been quoting. As far as I can find, he made no further use of it, either in the *Principles* or in *Industry and Trade*.

II

In coming now to more recent thinking on the psychology of economic behaviour, it's convenient to distinguish two aspects: the motivational (corresponding to animal spirits) and the cognitive (corresponding to the response to uncertainty). The two interact in the way I've been describing.

First, motivation.

Marshall's remarks don't relate exclusively or even primarily to business investment. The same can be said of the modern economist whose ideas have most in common with Marshall's, Scitovsky. Scitovsky was writing mainly about consumption, but his ideas can quite well be applied to business behaviour as well.[5]

He distinguished between comfort and pleasure. He related both to arousal, which he understood in a quite strictly physiological sense, relating to the stimulation of the cortex. In this he was drawing on the writings of psychologists of the 1960s, especially Daniel Berlyne. Roughly speaking, Scitovsky's idea is that comfort is a function of the level of arousal and pleasure is a function of the rate of change of arousal, and arousal in turn depends on stimulus. Arousal increases when something is going on: in the absence of ups and downs in arousal you may be comfortable but it's boring. The same idea was expressed, in more cynical form, in an alleged cocktail party aphorism of Frank Knight. 'Tell me, Professor Knight', he was asked, 'what is it you think that people really want in life?' He replied: 'Trouble'.

Arousal in Scitovsky performs the same function as 'activity' does in Marshall. Arousal leads to activity and activity leads to arousal. Keynes and Marshall, Knight and Scitovsky, represent a family of theories rather than a single theory. There are differences between them. What they have in common is the hypothesis that the motive to economic behaviour arises from doing as well as having, from becoming as well as being. The ultimate reason could lie in genetic evolution: it is functional to be stimulated to action in certain circumstances, and the arousal mechanism evolved accordingly in *Homo sapiens*, as in other animals. It could further be held that the general arousal mechanism, once implanted, has made people respond to a variety of stimuli, including some quite different from those for which the mechanism was functional in the prehistory when evolution was taking place.

I said doing as well as being. As well as, not instead of. It would be absurd to write off the conventional kind of economic motivation. In fact, the two kinds can interact in interesting ways. For example, if

---

[5] Scitovsky (1977 and 1981).

the system is formalised in Scitovsky's manner, in terms of both the level of a variable (arousal), determining comfort, and its rate of change, affecting pleasure, cycles can result. Karl Marx's model of the trade cycle can be interpreted in that way: the capitalists' urge to accumulate propels the upswing until it's brought to a halt by the adverse effect on their comfort caused by the resulting fall in the rate of profit.

Any form of hypothesis that attributes pleasure to activity or (still more) to novelty has an element of paradox. It requires to be reconciled with such widespread views as that people dislike having to make up their minds and that they are hostile to change and that the chief reward of monopoly is a quiet life. A number of possible reconciliations may be offered, not inconsistent with one another. It may be a matter of degree, too much stimulation and too little both being disagreeable (Wundt's Law).[6] Or it may be a matter of personality differences, some people being more plentifully endowed with animal spirits than others. Or a distinction may exist between (alarming) change imposed from outside and (interesting) change initiated by oneself.[7]

How does this kind of theory, if valid, affect the theory of investment? Investment is a means of changing things, and as such is a non-routine activity. It satisfies the procreant urge, gives an outlet to the animal spirits. Hence it is capable of being a source of satisfaction in itself, independently of its actual consequences. Does this mean simply that investment is in part a consumer good, conferring a non-pecuniary utility? If so, the theoretical consequences are not particularly radical, even though the presence of this non-pecuniary utility will affect the outcome. Its effect is like that of a subsidy to investment. But there are also more radical implications.

In the first place, in so far as the non-pecuniary utility is a function of change, a stationary equilibrium is precluded, at least for the individual economic agent.

[6] Scitovsky (1977), pp. 34–5.
[7] Two supporting findings may be cited for this distinction, one from social psychology, the other from experimental psychology. (1) Decision-making has been found to be unpleasantly stressful only if all available options look likely to involve loss (Janis and Mann (1977), chapter 1). This condition will not be fulfilled in the case of self-initiated changes, since there the option exists of keeping the status quo. (2) Rats, as is well known, will work to administer electrical stimulation to the so-called 'pleasure centres' of the brain. However, they have been found to work to prevent the stimulation when it is recorded and played back to them under the control of the experimenter. Steiner *et al.* (1969), pp. 90–1.

In the second place, although people's tastes may remain constant in the sense that they always have a need for arousal, there are systematic forces operating to prevent constancy in their tastes as expressed in action. Having achieved one thing, they seek a new goal.

Indeed the question how their energies are channelled indicates that the theory is in need of supplementation. The underlying psychological theory is not a theory of investment as such, although it's capable of being applied to investment. In the language of Descartes, the animal spirits are always in motion but the will directs them. What determines the direction in which it channels them? People set themselves tasks and get a kick out of the effort to achieve them. But what determines the tasks they set themselves? Business expansion by means of gross fixed capital formation is only one of the ways in which an outlet may be sought for the procreant urge, even among those in a position to undertake it. Altogether different outlets might be chosen. People might find their outlet in purely speculative activity, or in the pursuit of personal promotion within a bureaucratic hierarchy, or simply in making money as an end in itself by whatever means serve best. Or else their self-imposed tasks might lie in some entirely non-economic field – politics or community activity or sport. If animal spirits are to be invoked in the explanation of economic behaviour, it becomes an important matter, separate from the underlying psychological idea, to determine what forces channel them. This is likely to depend to a significant extent on the cultural environment, hence, obviously, creating scope for differences between countries and periods. It will also depend on individuals' personalities. That in turn will again depend partly on the cultural environment, in so far as a given organisation of society causes people with a particular temperament to get into a position where investment decisions fall to them. Such non-random selection of individuals for jobs makes inter-personal differences in channelling likely to be a more important complication in the application of arousal theories to business (or political) decisions than to consumption decisions – everyone is a consumer, albeit not on an equal scale, but not everyone is called on to make substantial investment decisions. I shall have more to say about channelling presently.

What basis for the whole approach is provided by psychologists? As far as I have been able to ascertain, the answer from the more rigorous, physiological, kind of psychological research is rather unsatisfactory. Psychologists appear to have been more successful in refuting broad theories of motivation than they have been in devising one that commands general support. We know that Descartes was very far from the mark. The nineteenth-century German psychologists referred to by Marshall in his footnotes are now largely forgotten. The more recently developed theory of generalised 'drive' was found to be open to serious objections.[8] The same, unfortunately, seems to have happened to some extent to the arousal theories used by Scitovsky. They have been found to contain an element of truth but they have less all-embracing application than was supposed in the 1960s. The motivational state, it appears, is a complex one, made up of a number of elements that are not too well correlated with one another. Psychologists have identified various behavioural regularities, but the reasons for them are not too well understood.[9]

These findings suggest that we should be chary of trying to explain too much by a single grand theory of motivation. However, it is not disputed that animals (and hence probably *Homo sapiens*) do work for stimulation and that novelty is a source of stimulation. It is also agreed that the motivational state is largely conditioned by society, both in respect of what we seek to do and of how we seek to do it. Influences of the kind discussed by Marshall, Keynes, Knight, and Scitovsky are therefore by no means precluded and may well be important. Whether it is best to conceptualise all such influences as alternative, substitutable, sources of arousal is more debatable. Just as it would be straining language to regard the procreant urge (in its literal sexual sense) in this way, so also it may be more appropriate to regard other impulses, of a kind more relevant to economics, as genetically implanted in their own right, with arousal an incidental feature only. Perhaps most prominent among such impulses are aggression and the desire for victory as an end in itself – apparent in many economic contexts, some of them capable of affecting investment: in takeover bids and in debates in the board room, as well as in industrial relations.

Behavioural and social psychologists, as well as physiological ones, exhibit lack of agreement on motivation. However, there is a fair amount of support for hypotheses couched, like the hypothesis of animal spirits, in terms of activity. At the most general level, one leading writer recently went so far as to say 'our utilities for ways of getting things are normally much higher than our utilities for the

[8] Hinde (1960).   [9] For a survey see Bolles (1975).

goods themselves' and he asked 'when people take action in order to achieve certain objectives, do they really know whether they are going to like what they get when they get it?'[10] The general notion can be related to a number of more specific ones: satisficing, enquiring, and goal ambiguity.

In so far as *satisficing* is taken as a theory of utility (rather than as a theory of search), it implies the choice of an objective, with utility being derived from progress towards that objective, whatever it may be. Once the objective is attained, a new one is chosen. The successive choice of objectives is equivalent to channelling, and it may be subject to forces of culture and personality, not to say arbitrariness.

An interesting expression of the equivalent to satisficing, as a theory of utility, is the model that has been put forward by the psychologists Kahneman and Tversky under the heading of prospect theory. The model was designed to explain the apparently anomalous attitudes towards risk exhibited by subjects in laboratory tests.[11] According to this model people value outcomes with reference to a base-point. At the base-point, there is a kink in their valuation function. For outcomes above the base-point, the valuation function is concave, in the conventional manner, but for outcomes below the base-point, it is convex. The base-point can be interpreted as the goal set by the satisficer. He does not set much store by doing better than that. He minds very much if he fails to reach it. He is diminishingly sensitive to larger shortfalls, on the principle that a miss is as good as a mile. In the limiting case, his valuation curve might reduce to a step function, with only two levels of utility, one for success and the other for failure. How he values any given outcome thus depends on his self-selected objective. Scope exists for important differences in the valuation set by different people on the same outcome, according to how high they set their sights.

In so far as this is the sort of way people behave, it helps one understand the first question commonly put by management consultants to their clients: What are your objectives? To an economist, this seems rather an odd question: one wonders whether firms can really differ much in their answers. But if objectives are self-selected, the question makes sense. The notion of self-selected objectives has something in common with the idea of activity as enquiry, put

---

[10] Kahneman in Ungson and Braunstein (eds.) (1982), p. 122.
[11] Kahneman and Tversky (1979).

forward by the clinical psychologist Kelly, who saw the motivation of the economic agent as similar to that of the research scientist, for whom the exact field of his research is of secondary importance.[12]

The management consultant's question is posed in awareness of the possibility also of *goal ambiguity*, another concept prominent in the behavioural literature.[13] If an individual or an organisation is subject to goal ambiguity, yet remains active, it would appear that activity has become an end in itself even more than under satisficing. On this reckoning, goal ambiguity is not necessarily a bad state of affairs – though if those concerned were not conscious of the ambiguity of their goals, the management consultant's question may help to clear their minds.

I have been speaking of the motivation of individuals or organisations, without distinguishing the two. Naturally, the collection of people into organisations does introduce fresh considerations. Proper discussion of those lies outside the scope of this paper. However, for present purposes, the differences may not be too important in principle; both individuals and organisations are capable, in their different ways, of being motivated by activity as such and of developing goals to guide that activity.

A hypothesis that does come into a rather different category from those I am discussing is one version of the so-called managerial theory of investment, based on the separation of ownership and control. This is the hypothesis that managers choose policies for their companies with a view to the maximisation of their own personal earnings, to the possible disregard of the interests of shareholders. This has nothing to do with animal spirits (though the effects of the two may be difficult to distinguish from each other in practice). It is simply an example of the principal-agent problem. As such it is a matter of institutions rather than psychology. Psychology comes in only in so far as the managers are deceiving themselves – persuading themselves that their plans are in the shareholders' interests when they are really just in their own.

The reference to self-deception takes me conveniently from the motivational aspects of economic psychology to the cognitive aspects.

---

[12] Kelly (1955). I owe this reference to Earl (1984) where the application of Kelly's ideas to economics is discussed and developed.   [13] March (1978).

III

The role assigned to cognition in textbook economics is Humean: cognition is and ought to be the slave of motivation. Keynes, in effect, made two observations on this. First, in the matter of investment decisions, the slave is given an impossible task, because the future is unknowable. Secondly, the slave is prone to do a bad job, by telling his master only what he wants to hear. The two observations are, I must say, not wholly consistent: if the job is impossible, who can say whether it is done well or badly? But this need not prevent us from asking how the slave does do his job.

Let me first note in parenthesis one cognitive implication of activity theories of motivation. That is to downgrade the importance of expectations. The immediate question for any decision-maker is: what shall I do? It is not: how do I think the future will unfold? How far he chooses to address himself to the second question as a preliminary to answering the first depends, amongst other things, on his motive for action. If the motive is purely consequentialist, expectations are of the essence. If it is not, he may quite reasonably take action without having formed any very explicit expectation about the future at all. Most obviously is this so if activity is purely an end in itself. If it is directed to some self-selected goal, he will certainly want to take a view on whether that goal looks likely to be attained, but he will not project further than that. The academic analyst may find it convenient to say that people behave *as if* they had certain expectations, but that should not be mistaken for a description of their actual thought processes. It is noteworthy that in the case of investment decisions, where firms often do make explicit projections, the projections are customarily made at a different and lower level of the organisation than the level where the actual decisions are arrived at. One may question how firmly the decision-makers really believe in the projections of their staff. They may well not be in a position to assess the validity of the projections anyway.

On cognition more generally, the starting point for much of the recent discussion among the economists has been Simon's concept of bounded rationality: perfect rationality is a chimera, because no one possesses the mental powers to marshal in his head all the information relevant to a difficult decision. The relevance of bounded rationality is not confined to situations characterised by Knightian uncertainty. The situation may just be too complicated to grasp comprehensively. Chess provides an example. But there is a good reason why bounded rationality should be particularly important under uncertainty. Situations where there is certainty or where uncertainty takes only the form of exactly calculable risk are in principle *simple*, in that the amount of information needed for action is limited. The thought needed may therefore lie well within the bounds of our rationality. It is easy, therefore, to understand the force of Keynes's idea that mental processes undergo some alteration if the cloud of uncertainty dissolves: the entrepreneur then need not hesitate to turn arbitrageur. Even if the situation is complicated, the amount of information that is required is still limited – if necessary the decision-maker can hire an actuary or other such expert to give him advice. But, in the case of Knightian uncertainty, there is no limit to the information that *might* turn out to be relevant – you could go on collecting it for ever. Even if you did, it would be pointless, because the boundedness of your rationality would prevent you from using it all.

The existence of bounded rationality means that we are liable to make mistakes. It does not as such mean that the mistakes have a systematic tendency to be in one direction rather than another. However, psychologists have also accumulated a good deal of evidence to suggest that our rationality is in certain respects systematically twisted, not merely bounded.[14] This evidence admittedly comes largely from laboratory tests on volunteer subjects, who have nothing real at stake; it's reasonable to argue that some of the biases observed would not apply to important business decisions that will be preceded by careful deliberation on the part of intelligent people. Examples include various tendencies to elementary fallacies about the laws of probability. That sort of mistake is not too difficult to avoid, given experience or time for thought (it is avoided by even moderately skilful bridge players). On the other hand, the potential fallacies are not so neatly isolated for identification in business decisions as they are in bridge; and many decisions do have to be made under great pressure.[15]

---

[14] Tversky and Kahneman (1974); Einhorn and Hogarth in Ungson and Braunstein (eds.) (1982).
[15] An entertaining and vivid account is in Mintzberg (1975). 'Despite the widespread use of capital budgeting procedures . . . executives in my study made a great many authorisations on an *ad hoc* basis. Apparently, many projects cannot wait or simply do not have the quantifiable costs and benefits that capital budgeting requires' (pp. 58–9).

Furthermore, a number of apparent systematic errors have been identified by psychologists that are not of this relatively trivial kind. We apparently have a tendency, for example, to give excessive weight to evidence that is immediately within our personal experience: thus even persons who are perfectly aware that statistical evidence has shown interviews to be very unreliable continue to attach a lot of importance to interviews conducted by themselves. This is a rather obvious example of boundedness in our rationality, a form of boundedness that is easy to identify in theory but evidently difficult to correct in practice. In the same category, and more directly connected with investment decisions, comes our apparent tendency to underestimate the overall likelihood of failure of a project that has many independent sources of possible failure, none of them perhaps very likely by itself. Unwise attempts at over-large leaps in technology come to mind in this connection.

In speaking of apparent cognitive failings, I have been careful to keep reiterating 'apparent'. What constitutes rationality (including attitude to risk) is conditional on objectives and circumstances. For example, if you are engaged in repeated plays, it is rational to value the probability p of an outcome x at an amount equal to p times the valuation you would set on x if it were the certain outcome. But in relation to one-off matters like investment decisions, it is not necessarily irrational to set a separate valuation on the degree of certainty as such, as experimental subjects apparently do.[16]

It is a much discussed and open question among behavioural theorists how far the appearance of cognitive failings reflects simply a wrong identification by the observer of people's objectives.[17] This applies both to apparent systematic biases and to the choice of how to allocate the limited amount of attention that our bounded rationality makes available. It is not disputed that rationality is bounded, and that mistakes will be made. But one can choose, in the light of one's objectives, where to be most careful to avoid them.

Our objectives may even in some cases dictate the commission of cognitive errors as such. Take the kind of errors analysed by the psychologists' theory of cognitive dissonance.[18] According to this theory, we have some degree of choice over the things that we choose to consider and hence over the beliefs that we choose to hold. It is

[16] Kahneman and Tversky (1979).
[17] March and Shiapira in Ungson and Braunstein (eds.) (1982).
[18] Festinger (1957); Akerlof and Dickens (1982).

disagreeable to contemplate evidence that militates against the soundness of some interesting idea we've had for action or some past idea that we've currently been acting on. So we are reluctant to devote as much thought to it as we are to thoughts about evidence tending to conform our own rightness. We are in love with our own ideas. Related to this, though not quite identical, is the suggestion that we take particular pains to avoid a decision we may regret if it should prove to have been wrong, because the regret will be a source of disutility in itself in addition to the disutility caused by the ill-effects of the decision.[19] This particular consideration is often quoted as an example of bureaucratic malfunction – the desire to avoid demonstrable error. But it can also occur within the mind of an individual. Cognitive dissonance can be regarded as rational if self-esteem or the avoidance of regret are included in the utility function. Admittedly some doubt is cast on this interpretation by the finding, established in a famous experiment on visual perception, that faulty adherence to ideas once they have been formed occurs even in situations where emotions are not involved.[20] But for many purposes the outcome will be the same on either interpretation.

Cognitive dissonance is not, as such, a reason for undertaking enterprises. But it is a reason for not giving them up. The implied mulishness may seem rather a far cry from the procreant urge. However, single-mindedness is often cited as one of the most important entrepreneurial attributes, and single-mindedness and mulishness are perhaps not too far apart.

If cognitive errors do occur systematically, the question arises why they are not eliminated by competition in a Darwinian manner.

One possible answer is that in certain circumstances they may actually be functional. Keynes's reference to the healthy man dismissing from his mind the thought of death conveys a suggestion that you won't make a good job of anything if you are perpetually pondering the possible objections. Given the limitations of our reasoning capacity and our energy, resolution and devotion may be the key elements in success, and in the nature of things, they must involve some disregard of the pale cast of thought. Most babies, by definition, are nothing out of the ordinary, but adequate child care requires that their parents should think they are. Cognitive error may serve a higher rationality.

[19] Loomes and Sugden (1982).   [20] Bruner and Potter (1964).

Much the same consideration may apply to the allocation of functions within the economy between individuals with differing personalities. Energy may come in joint supply with proneness to make mistakes. Steady men who avoid cognitive errors may have a tendency to lack the forcefulness needed to run a rapidly expanding business. Darwinism selects for relative fitness, not for absolute fitness, and paragons are not usually available.

More broadly, it may be the case that, given our bounded rationality, the best that we can do is to adopt modes of thought that in general lead to better results than alternative ones, even though they may lead to less good results in certain types of situation. (This is similar to Lucas's idea in macro-economics that cyclical fluctuations may be part of the price of allocative efficiency in so far as misperceptions of absolute prices are an unavoidable concomitant of alertness to relative prices.) The extent to which this happens will depend on the extent to which we are free to adapt our modes of thinking to particular circumstances. This in turn will depend on how far we are free to choose our modes of thought and how far they are ingrained in us genetically.

The conclusions of psychological and behavioural studies, as they bear on the animal spirits hypothesis, can therefore be summed up briefly as follows. There is good reason to suppose that people are motivated, in part, by the satisfaction they get from activity as such, particularly activity towards a self-selected goal. Goals lie in the future and the future is uncertain; so the connection with uncertainty is inherent. Our objectives are liable to have an effect on our cognitive processes and on our attitudes towards risk, both for rational reasons and for irrational ones.

It remains now to consider the application of these general psychological ideas more specifically to investment.

IV

It is one thing to show that certain interesting psychological propensities exist, another to show that they are important quantitatively. I should not wish to deny that conventional economic reasoning can explain much about investment. Moreover there is a familiar methodological problem. Even if behavioural evidence establishes that people persistently think and act in a certain way – which can scarcely be claimed in the present instance – it is almost always possible to devise some way of arguing that it really amounts indirectly to profit-maximisation, despite appearances to the contrary. In the case of the animal spirits hypothesis, a further difficulty is that it can take a variety of forms. For example, animal spirits may operate persistently, or alternatively they may be subject to periodical checks in the Marxian manner as they are brought up against reality, so that their effect cancels out in the long run.

Let's consider the hypothesis that they operate consistently. The standard kind of econometric investment function is not very helpful as a test, because models of that kind are usually concerned to explain fluctuations in investment, or intersectoral differences in investment, rather than its average level. This applies even to the class of model most closely akin to the Keynesian one, in which investment is expressed as a function of the valuation ratio (Tobin's q), that is to say the ratio of the market value of a company's equity to the value of its physical assets, or, equivalently, the ratio of the profit rate on its assets to the yield on shares. On *any* reckoning one would expect a positive correlation between fluctuations in the valuation ratio and fluctuations in investment, and so it turns out. More relevant in the present context is the absolute level of the valuation ratio. On orthodox theory one would expect it to average around unity, or perhaps slightly above unity so as to provide an inducement to positive investment. How this is affected by animal spirits in the sense of optimism depends on the exact assumptions made. I do not propose now to go into the algebra of possible alternative cases. However, there are reasonable assumptions one can make that lead to the conclusion that one might expect intuitively, namely that either optimism in the minds of managers or (a different point) greater optimism in the minds of managers than in the collective mind of the stock market will tend to make for an equilibrium valuation ratio below unity.

Unfortunately, statistical calculation of the valuation ratio in the relevant sense turns out to be far from straightforward. Non-trivial complications are introduced by such causes as inflation, corporate taxation, exclusion of land and goodwill from the book value of assets, and arbitrariness in the estimate of depreciation. By the time attempts have been made to adjust for these, one is not left with much faith in the reliability of the *absolute* levels shown for the valuation ratio, though its fluctuations are no doubt tracked well enough. For what they are worth, the figures for the United Kingdom in the last

twenty-five years or so come out about equally often above and below
unity.[21] They have been below unity for most of the past ten years,
during which none the less positive net capital formation is recorded.
But overall the result must be considered quite indecisive, neither
confirming the animal spirits hypothesis nor refuting it.

Since this attempt at a direct test proves unhelpful, I shall
enumerate a few phenomena to which the animal spirits hypothesis
may be relevant, while conceding that for almost all of them attempts
have been or can be made to devise explanations of a more orthodox
kind.

The first is the fact, too well known to require documentation, that
firms finance a large proportion of their investment out of ploughed-
back profits. Possible explanations can be sought from the effects of
transactions costs and information costs and in some cases tax
considerations. But the phenomenon is also compatible with firms
being systematically more optimistic about their prospects than the
market is. One may look at the question from the other side and ask
why companies, if they do decide not to distribute all their earnings,
choose to plough the profits back in their own expansion rather than
buying shares in other companies, or gilt-edged, or property, or
whatever. On the face of it, that would be the more profitable thing to
do for the many companies that have a valuation ratio persistently
below unity. Force is added to the question by the fact that buying a
general portfolio of financial assets is exactly what companies do with
their pension funds. Why do the interests of their pensioners call for a
different use of funds from the interests of their shareholders? Of
course, buying exclusively financial assets would not work if everyone
did it, because ultimately there would be no business to hold equities
in, but there would be no need to go to that length. Companies do
indeed hold financial assets, and conglomerates acquire portfolios of
real assets that are very widespread. But holding shares in other
companies is still not regarded as the normal practice for a trading
company.

Unless a company is in difficulties, it typically regards it as
axiomatic that it should carry out replacement investment when
necessary, and moreover that it should finance it internally –
otherwise the equity is being diluted. A similar consideration may
underlie some of the internal financing of new investment as well.

---

[21] Jenkinson (1981).

That consideration is concern about the company's share of its market. A common belief in business is that, if you do not retain your share of the market, you're on the way out, even if your sales remain constant absolutely. This then raises the question why staying in business itself is regarded as so axiomatic. If you could get a better result from holding financial assets, you might do better to *let* the business run down. Reluctance to go along that path suggests the possibility of cognitive dissonance.

The remaining applications I shall mention involve the question of channelling.

The first relates to cycles. There is no inherent reason why people should not get a kick out of the sort of non-routine activity that consists of identifying loss-making elements in a company and closing them down. Particularly is this so if the people are newcomers to the business and free from emotional ties to it. In recent years this outlet for energies has been at a premium and the expansionist outlet has been at a discount. This suggests a possible source of over-shooting. Trends in expansion or retrenchment, which are themselves appropriate to surrounding economic conditions, or even enforced by them, may become exaggerated; not only because they create a climate of opinion, but also because they bring to the fore in company management individuals who are predisposed by their personalities or by their professional background to find job satisfaction in moving the company in the one direction or the other, as the case may be.

The effects of inter-personal differences in channelling may be observed also in the life-cycle of the individual firm. It has been common for the expansion phase in the life of a firm to be dominated by a single personality at its head, someone with strong expansionist impulses. This person in the end overreaches. His successors have different personalities and different objectives. It falls to them to reorganise and rationalise and, in some cases, cut back.[22]

Both in the business cycle and in the life-cycle of the firm, changes in policy may occur, without any change in management, from changes in the amount of influence wielded by creditors, especially banks. The firm's leaders and its bankers have different objective functions in relation to its operations. If it runs into cash flow problems, increasing weight will come to attach to the view of people whose animal spirits are not engaged in it. The point is not that bank

---

[22] Silberston in Currie *et al.* (eds.) (1981).

officials necessarily are lacking in animal spirits, but, rather, that they find a different outlet for them (acquiring Crocker National Bank, say).

Finally, an example relative to trends over longer periods and the possible influence of institutional change. In considering long-run trends in British investment, my collaborators and I have commented on the following curious phenomenon.[23] Over the century or so up to 1973, the profit rate fell very substantially relative to the interest rate; yet investment, as a proportion of income, did not fall as might have been expected, but actually rose. That might appear to suggest a progressive *rise* in animal spirits, contrary to the normal stereotype of trends in British entrepreneurship. In our book, we attributed this surprising phenomenon mainly to a progressive reduction in capital market imperfections. But one could also postulate a change in the channelling of animal spirits in consequence of an increased separation of ownership from control.[24] The argument would be that the managers of a public company are officials, people of relatively little account financially apart from their company, so that the only outlet they can share for their animal spirits is in the company's success and expansion. By contrast, the old-fashioned entrepreneur, once he had succeeded in business, could if he chose, without having to consult anyone else, transfer his animal spirits to some other sphere of activity altogether, by building up a country estate or acquiring race horses or going into parliament. Similar speculations suggest themselves about possible consequences of institutional differences that exist between countries rather than over time. A different channelling of animal spirits may be expected according to whether executives are mobile between companies, as in the US, or stay with one company for a lifetime, as in Japan.

V

A few remarks in conclusion. Neglect of the psychological forces that I have been discussing is a lacuna in conventional economic theory. At the same time, there are some qualifications. Neither all the non-

[23] Matthews, Feinstein, and Odling-Smee (1982), pp. 359–61.
[24] A cross-section finding consistent with this is that owner-controlled companies on average appear to earn a higher profit rate than management-controlled companies. Nyman and Silberston (1978). Both this and the trend noted in the text could, of course, be attributed to managerial personal income-maximisation.

consequentialist motivations nor all the cognitive biases will necessarily be of quite the type described by Keynes as animal spirits, significant though that type be. Perhaps more important, it is doubtful how far it is right to relate the effect of these psychological considerations so exclusively to investment in physical capital as a reading of Keynes might suggest. One would certainly wish to extend it at least to takeovers; and one might conjecture that animal spirits play a part in the motivation of both physical investment and of takeovers, but that the choice between these two modes of expansion, with their potentially different macro-consequences, is largely, though not necessarily wholly, determined by rational calculation of the kind familiar in economics. The broad idea should also be extended to other forms of investment, such as investment in human capital and investment in the development of new products and new processes. Such an extension might be helpful in the explanation of technical change and productivity growth, which we have actually been a good deal less successful in modelling by conventional theories than we have with investment. But almost all economic decisions, except the most routine ones, have long drawn out effects in the future and thus involve uncertainty; and almost all non-routine activities are a potential source of stimulus. The wider-ranging the possible outlets for animal spirits, the more pervasive are their possible effects. The greater, too, is the potential importance of shifts between outlets over time and, hence, the greater is the importance of understanding the forces that bring about those shifts.

References

Akerlof, G.A. and Dickens, W.T. (1982), 'The Economic Consequences of Cognitive Dissonance', *American Economic Review*, 72: 307–19.

Arrow, K.J. (1982), 'Risk Perception in Psychology and Economics', *Economic Inquiry*, 20: 1–9.

Bolles, R.C. (1975), *Theory of Motivation*, 3rd edn, New York: Harper and Row.

Bruner, J.S. and Potter, M.C. (1964), 'Interference in Visual Recognition', *Science*, 144: 424–5.

Earl, P.E. (1984), 'A Behavioural Analysis of Choice', Cambridge University Ph.D. Dissertation.

Einhorn, H.J. and Hogarth, R.M. (1982), 'Behavioural Decision Theory: Processes of Judgement and Choice', in G.R. Ungson and D.N. Braunstein (eds.).

Festinger, L. (1957), *A Theory of Cognitive Dissonance*, Stanford: Stanford University Press.

Hawtrey, R.G. (1926), *The Economic Problem*, London: Longmans, Green & Co.

Hinde, R.A. (1960), 'Critique of Energy Models of Motivation', *Symposium of the Society for Experimental Biology*, vol. 14: 199–213.

Hume, D. (1739), *A Treatise of Human Nature*, Oxford University Press.

Janis, I.L. and Mann, L. (1977), *Decision Making*, New York: Free Press.

Jenkinson, N.H. (1981), 'Investment, Profitability and the Valuation Ratio', *Bank of England Discussion Paper*, no. 17.

Kahn, R.F. (1984), *The Making of Keynes' General Theory*, Cambridge University Press.

Kahneman, D. (1982), 'Bureaucracies, Minds, and the Human Engineering of Decisions', in G.R. Ungson and D.N. Braunstein (eds.).

Kahneman, D. and Tversky, A. (1979), 'Prospect Theory: An Analysis of Decisions Under Risk', *Econometrica*, 47: 263–91.

Kelly, G.A. (1955), *The Psychology of Personal Constructs*, New York: Norton.

Keynes, J.M. (1921), *A Treatise on Probability*, London: Macmillan.
  (1936), *The General Theory of Employment, Interest and Money*, London: Macmillan.
  (1937), 'The General Theory of Employment', *The Quarterly Journal of Economics*, 51: 209–2.
  The Collected Writings of John Maynard Keynes, vols. 13 (1973) and 27 (1980), edited by D. Moggridge, London: Macmillan.

Lavington, F. (1922), *The Trade Cycle*, London: P.S. King and Son.

Loomes, G. and Sugden, R. (1982), 'Regret Theory: An Alternative Theory of Rational Choice Under Uncertainty', *Economic Journal*, 92. 805–24.

March, J.G. (1978), 'Bounded Rationality, Ambiguity, and the Engineering of Choice', *The Bell Journal of Economics*, 9: 587–608.

March, J.G. and Shiapira, Z. (1982), 'Behavioural Decision Theory and Organizational Decision Theory', in G.R. Ungson and D.N. Braunstein (eds.).

Marshall, A. (1890), *Principles of Economics* (1st edn.), London: Macmillan.
  (1919), *Industry and Trade*, London: Macmillan.

Matthews, R.C.O., Feinstein, C.H. and Odling-Smee, J.C. (1982), *British Economic Growth, 1856–1973*, Oxford: Clarendon Press.

Mintzberg, H. (1975), 'The Manager's Job: Folklore and Fact', *Harvard Business Review*, vol. 53, July–August: 49–61.

Munby, A.N.L. (1975), 'The Book Collector', in Milo Keynes (ed.), *Essays on John Maynard Keynes*, Cambridge University Press.

Nyman, S. and Silberston, A. (1978), 'The Ownership and Control of Industry', *Oxford Economic Papers*, n.s., 30: 74–101.

Robertson, D.H. (1915), *A Study of Industrial Fluctuation*, London: P.S. King & Son.

Robinson, J. (1962), *Essays in the Theory of Economic Growth*, London: Macmillan.

Scitovsky, T. (1977), *The Joyless Economy*, New York: Oxford University Press.

(1981), 'The Desire for Excitement in a Modern Society', *Kyklos*, 31: 3–13.

Silberston, A. (1981), 'Factors Affecting the Growth of the Firm – Theory and Practice', in D. Currie, D. Peel and W. Peters (eds.), *Microeconomic Analysis*, London: Croom Helm.

Steiner, S.S., Beer, B. and Shaffer, M.M. (1969), 'Escape from Self-Produced Rates of Brain Stimulation', *Science*, 163: 90–1.

Tversky, A. and D. Kahneman (1974), 'Judgement under Uncertainty; Heuristics and Biases', *Science*, 185: 1124–31.

Ungson, G.R. and Braunstein, D.N. (eds.) (1982), *Decision Making: An Interdisciplinary Inquiry*, Boston, Mass.:, Kent Publishing Company.

8   Keynes on the rationality of decision procedures under uncertainty: the investment decision*

GAY MEEKS

The future is yet to come (as an MP once solemnly informed the House of Commons). But indubitable though this claim may be, it can scarcely be said to furnish the kind of specific information about the prospects on which a man might base his detailed plans. What else do we know about the future course of events – know for certain, that is? Precious little, the Sceptics assure us, and much less than we tend to suppose. Suppose they are right: what then?

Keynes' treatment of this matter (especially in chapter 12 of *The General Theory*) forms the subject of this essay. The analysis will show Keynes as endorsing the sceptical claim that we cannot acquire sure knowledge of what will happen in the future and will present him as particularly concerned with just how, given this, economic agents do manage in practice to cope with the problems of (perhaps woefully) limited information about events to come. This much is of course common ground with such exponents of Keynes as Shackle (1967) and Minsky (1975), but the parallel with sceptical philosophy will be pressed further here and a more formal statement of Keynes' approach will be presented. As a result, a dimension of the argument that is missing from those accounts will be introduced and explored; for it emerges from the analysis that, crucial though Keynes thought the impact of uncertainty on our actions and especially our investment decisions to be, he did not view the resulting behaviour as unreasonable or (in an important sense) irrational – rather the reverse. From this perspective, he can be seen as stressing the role of some unreasoned elements in our decisions (as Shackle showed) and yet also as seeking to give a much-wanted account of economic

* This is a revised version of a paper first completed in 1976. I would like to thank Robin Carter, Phyllis Deane, Martin Hollis, Geoff Meeks, Joan Robinson, Amartya Sen and a number of Cambridge graduate students for their comments on an earlier draft; and I am grateful to the Calouste Gulbenkian Foundation and to the former Social Science Research Council for their support.

agents' *rational* response to conditions not just of risk but of gross uncertainty. But my attempt at a formal account and an assessment of Keynes' argument on this issue also draws attention to some difficulties in interpreting him: I hope to be able to explain some puzzling, even apparently contradictory, aspects of what he says.[1]

The strategy will be, first, to present a diagrammatic summary of what I believe Keynes' argument to be (section I); second, to support this by drawing together some of his own statements (section II); next, to relate his position briefly to its antecedents in Humean sceptical philosophy (section III); and then to weigh up the issues on which its success turns (section IV).

I

This section summarises what I believe to be Keynes' position on the general basis for our decisions about the future (and hence for our actions) and for investment decisions in particular, taking it to be represented by the following 'structure diagram',[2] accompanied by the 'dictionary' of propositions below. In such a diagram, the notation p ----→ q indicates not that p entails q but only that p is *held by the arguer* to be a ground for believing q. Letters in the diagram stand for propositions and the dictionary provides the key to them, so that diagram and dictionary are to be read together. The propositions relate both to Keynes' general argument about future-regarding decisions and to his specific one about investment: I've presented them side by side because he tends to switch about from one to the other (this dual argument is indeed the source of some of his perplexing remarks, to be taken up in section IV).

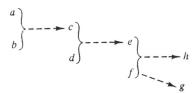

Figure 8.1/*Structure diagram of Keynes' argument*

[1] The idea that impulsive or conventional decisions might yet be rational under uncertainty according to Keynes has now entered into two doctoral theses at Cambridge that have since been published (see Carabelli, 1988 and O'Donnell, 1989) and into a colleague's argument (Lawson, 1985). But Keynes' claims about this still stand in need of some clarification and also demand to be debated. Some of the seeming confusions in his position were taken up but, I think, misinterpreted by Coddington (1976). [2] Following J.L. Mackie.

Dictionary to Figure 8.1

(a) It is impossible for us to deduce from our data what the future course of events will be; for instance, we cannot acquire (certain) knowledge, *ex ante*, of the future stream of returns from an investment.

(b) It is impossible for us to establish a quantitative probability for every possible future state of the world; in particular, we cannot measure satisfactorily the probabilities of the various possible future returns from a capital asset.

(c) Since actions have consequences in the future, we can deduce from our data neither which actions are best (given our goals), nor, in general, even which promise to be best; for example, if we are seeking to maximise profit, we face the difficulty that we cannot prove mathematically just from known facts or likelihoods which investment projects to favour.

(d) We have to act and to choose between possible courses of action; similarly, investing is imperative for society and decisions where to invest have to be made.

(e) In general, we must select a course of action by some means other than pure deduction from our data; and again this applies to the investment decision.

(f) In practice our method of choosing actions is routine, in the sense that in the last analysis we rely on a set of habits and conventions (following the crowd) and especially on the custom of assuming that the future will be like the present and recent past; for example, the entrepreneur of an unquoted company assumes for practical purposes that the yield he expects from an investment project on the basis of the present state of affairs will in fact accrue, whilst those investing in the financial sense, on the stock market, assume in practice that the market's existing valuations give a largely correct guide to future prospects.

(g) Since the basis for decision is of this merely conventional kind, subjective factors – including temperament, fashion, and maybe even panic and hysteria – can readily exert an influence, and in markets speculation is likely to arise; thus, the extent to which the entrepreneur of an unquoted company will invest may depend partly on impulse or his mood, and the stock market is subject to waves of optimism and pessimism.

(h) But even so, our method of judging how to act isn't unreasonable, given the circumstances of unavoidable uncertainty; in particular, in these circumstances and so long as the bulk of investment activity remains dependent on private initiative, the way in which that activity is pursued is as good as could reasonably be expected.

Summing this up, I'm taking Keynes to hold (in a simplified version) that (a) (premise) the future course of events cannot be known deductively; (b) (premise) nor in general forecast by means of a numerical theory of probability; so (c) as a rule investment decisions which are rational in neoclassical economists' standard sense of this term ('substantively' rational in Simon's (1976) useful terminology) are out; (d) (premise) yet decisions on investment have to be made; so (given (c)) (e) we make them non-deductively and, in general, without the aid of numerical probabilities; (f) (premise) relying in practice on habit and convention (in particular, on the custom of assuming that usually the future will be like the present and recent past); thus (g) (first conclusion) giving scope for mood and mass psychology to have considerable sway; but also (given (e)) (h) (second conclusion) not acting unreasonably or (in the appropriate wide sense) irrationally, given the circumstances of unavoidable uncertainty.

Now I need to show what warrant there is for interpreting Keynes' position in this way.

II

In this section, the set of propositions just presented will be related to Keynes' own (probably familiar) words. I take the argument in three main stages.

(1) Propositions (a) and (b), leading to (c)

Perhaps Keynes' strongest assertion of premise (a) comes in his 1937 Galton Lecture to the Eugenics Society which opens with the words: 'the future never resembles the past – as we well know. But generally speaking, our imagination and our knowledge are too weak to tell us what particular changes to expect. We do not know what the future holds' (XIV, p. 124). Applying the point to the judging of investment prospects in *The General Theory*, Keynes tells us that 'the outstanding fact' about 'our estimates of prospective yield' is:

the extreme precariousness of the basis of knowledge on which [they] have to be made. Our knowledge of the factors which will govern the yield of an investment some years hence is usually very slight and often negligible. If we speak frankly, we have to admit that our basis of knowledge for estimating the yield ten years hence of a railway, a copper mine, a textile factory, the goodwill of a patent medicine, an Atlantic liner, a building in the City of London amounts to little and sometimes to nothing; or even five years hence.

(GT, pp. 149–50)[3]

Then in his QJE paper of 1937, Keynes went on to give as one of the two 'main grounds of [his] departure' from 'the traditional theory' the fact that 'the orthodox theory assumes that we have a knowledge of the future of a kind quite different from that which we actually possess'. He adds that 'this false rationalisation follows the lines of the Benthamite calculus'; and he believes the Benthamite error about the future comes in assuming it calculable: 'the hypothesis of a calculable future leads to a wrong interpretation of . . . [our] principles of behaviour' (XIV, p. 122). Here premise (b) becomes explicit, for Keynes pours scorn on the traditional practice according to which:

at any given time facts and expectations were assumed to be given in a definite and calculable form; and risks, of which, though admitted, not much notice was taken, were supposed to be capable of an exact actuarial computation. The calculus of probability, though mention of it was kept in the background, was supposed to be capable of reducing uncertainty to the same calculable status as that of certainty itself.   (XIV, pp. 112–13)

But 'actually', says Keynes, 'we have, as a rule, only the vaguest idea of any but the most direct consequences of our acts' (XIV, p. 113). Keynes views uncertainty, then, as intractable enough 'as a rule' to prevent us from making those calculations of wise action which demand that exact probabilities be assigned to the various possible outcomes; and he sees the difficulty as especially acute for the investment decision:

The whole object of the accumulation of wealth is to produce results, at a comparatively distant, and sometimes at an *indefinitely* distant date. Thus the fact that our knowledge of the future is fluctuating, vague and uncertain, renders wealth a peculiarly unsuitable subject for the methods of the classical

---

[3] In the references to Keynes' writings, the following abbreviations will be used: GT for *The General Theory of Employment, Interest and Money*; TP for *A Treatise on Probability*; roman numerals to indicate volumes of *The Collected Writings of John Maynard Keynes*, edited by Moggridge.

economic theory . . . By 'uncertain' knowledge, let me explain, I do not mean merely to distinguish what is known for certain from what is only probable. The game of roulette is not subject, in this sense, to uncertainty; nor is the prospect of a Victory bond being drawn. Or, again, the expectation of life is only slightly uncertain. Even the weather is only moderately uncertain. The sense in which I am using the term is that in which the prospect of a European war is uncertain, or the price of copper and the rate of interest twenty years hence, or the obsolescence of a new invention, or the position of private wealth owners in the social system in 1970. About these matters there is no scientific basis on which to form any calculable probability whatever. We simply do not know. (XIV, pp. 113–14)

Proposition (c) then finds expression in a passage which presents it as a consequence of the premises (a) and (b), thus summarising the whole of the first stage of the argument – the passage in which Keynes insists that 'human decisions affecting the future, whether personal or political or economic, cannot depend on strict mathematical expectation, since the basis for making such calculations does not exist' (GT, pp. 162–3).

(2)   Propositions (c), (d) and so (e)

The introduction of the idea of the 'need for action' and the 'necessity for decision' enables the next stage of the argument to proceed. For, if we are to decide between courses of action at all, as indeed (new premise (d)) we must, then, the 'ideal' calculus not being available (proposition (c)), we are forced to fall back on some cruder form of decision procedure – on the best means of judgement that are to hand (proposition (e)).

Keynes presents this line of reasoning several times. For example, having stressed in the context of investment that there are many aspects of the future about which 'we simply do not know', he immediately adds that 'nevertheless, the necessity for action and for decision compels us as practical men to do our best to overlook this awkward fact' (XIV, p. 114). Similarly, those principles of behaviour which Keynes believes the orthodox calculating theory interprets so wrongly are, he says, 'principles of behaviour which the need for action compels us to adopt' (XIV, p. 122). Or again, in the Galton Lecture, having told us once more that 'we do not know what the future holds', Keynes continues: 'Nevertheless, as living and moving beings we are forced to act. Peace and comfort of mind require that we should hide from ourselves how little we foresee. Yet we must be guided by some hypothesis' (XIV, p. 124). And in an early chapter of *The General Theory*, the argument is presented as encompassing virtually all production (i.e. as applying, in Keynes' terms, to short-term as well as long-term expectation):

> All production is for the purpose of ultimately satisfying a consumer. Time usually elapses, however – and sometimes much time – between the incurring of costs by the producer (with the consumer in view) and the purchase of the output by the ultimate consumer. Meanwhile, the entrepreneur (including both the producer and the investor in this description) has to form the best expectations he can as to what consumers will be willing to pay when he is ready to supply them (directly or indirectly) after the lapse of what may be a lengthy period; and he has no choice but to be guided by these expectations, if he is to produce at all by processes which occupy time.   (GT, p. 46)

(3)   *Propositions (e) and (f), whence (g) and (h)*

We have to 'form the best expectations [we] can', then; but on what basis do we manage even that? Having written in the Galton Lecture that 'we must be guided by some hypothesis', Keynes goes on: 'We tend, therefore, to substitute for the knowledge which is unattainable certain conventions, the chief of which is to assume, contrary to all likelihood, that the future will resemble the past. This is how we act in practice' (XIV, p. 124) (premise (f)). Elsewhere, he expands on this convention. 'Our usual practice', he writes, is 'to take the existing situation and to project it into the future, modified only to the extent that we have more or less definite reasons for expecting a change' (GT, p. 148). And again:

> We assume that the present is a much more serviceable guide to the future than a candid examination of past experience would show it to have been hitherto. In other words we largely ignore the prospect of future changes about the actual character of which we know nothing . . . We assume that the existing state of opinion as expressed in prices and the character of existing output is based on a *correct* summing up of the future prospects, so that we can accept it as such unless and until something new and relevant comes into the picture.   (XIV, p. 114)

And he also details another aspect of our resort to conventional judgements – the way in which we seem to suppose that there will be safety in numbers and accordingly try to take refuge in the crowd. With organised investment markets, 'we endeavour to fall back on the judgement of the rest of the world . . . to conform with the behaviour of the majority or average', so that there results 'a society of individuals each of whom is endeavouring to copy the others' (XIV, p. 114). These then are the means by which we manage, in Keynes' view, to '[save] our faces as rational, economic men' (XIV, p. 114).

But the third stage of the argument, incorporating this proposition that in practice our method of choosing actions is conventional and routine, involves two final moves – that from (f) to (g) and that from (f), given (e), to (h).

Take first the move from (f) to (g). To say that our actual method of making future-regarding decisions is in the main merely conventional is to allow, Keynes holds, that the decisions themselves will strictly speaking lack 'an adequate or secure foundation' (XIV, p. 118), however reassuring such a method may feel. For instance, when we project the existing situation into the future, this means that 'the facts of the existing situation enter, in a sense disproportionately, into the formation of our long-term expectations' (GT, p. 148). And yet organised investment markets have been able to develop, with tacit reliance just on the maintenance of this convention of assuming that things will continue as they are, 'a convention, in an absolute view of things so arbitrary' (GT, p. 153; see also GT, pp. 152 and 162).

But it is the fact that our actual, conventional basis for judgements about the future *is* inevitably weak which opens the way for other factors (such as mood, fashion, speculation, sometimes panic and hysteria) to exert an influence on our expectations, and so on our decisions (proposition (g)). This is the cue for some of the most famous passages in *The General Theory*, as Keynes explains that in these conditions the entrepreneur's willingness to embark on investment projects becomes in part dependent upon 'animal spirits'. 'If human nature felt no temptation to take a chance', he writes, 'no satisfaction (profit apart) in constructing a factory, a railway, a mine or a farm, there might not be much investment merely as a result of cold calculation' (GT, p. 150). Indeed, it is:

characteristic of human nature that a large proportion of our positive activities depend on spontaneous optimism rather than on a mathematical expectation, whether moral or hedonistic or economic. Most, probably, of our decisions to do something positive, the full consequences of which will be drawn out over many days to come, can only be taken as a result of animal spirits – of a spontaneous urge to action rather than inaction, and not as the outcome of a weighted average of quantitative benefits multiplied by quantitative probabilities. Enterprise only pretends to itself to be mainly actuated by the statements in its own prospectus, however candid and sincere. Only a little more than an expedition to the South Pole, is it based on an exact calculation of benefits to come. Thus if the animal spirits are dimmed and the spontaneous optimism falters, leaving us nothing to depend on but a mathematical expectation, enterprise will fade and die.   (GT, p. 162)

'This means,' he continues, ' . . . that economic prosperity is excessively dependent on a political and social atmosphere which is congenial to the average business man' and that 'in estimating the prospects of investment, we must have regard . . . to the nerves and hysteria and even the digestions and reactions to the weather of those upon whose spontaneous activity it largely depends' (GT, p. 162).

And just as individual psychological responses gain leverage on entrepreneurs' decisions to invest, so also 'mass psychology' affects stock market behaviour (GT, p. 170). Again the argument here is well known. An entrepreneur about to make an investment cannot know for sure what its prospects are going to be, but all the same he may well have more idea on the subject than the man in the street will do, and so, reasons Keynes, with the growth of investment markets 'the element of real knowledge in the valuation of investments by those who own them or contemplate purchasing them has seriously declined' (GT, p. 153). And:

A conventional valuation which is established as the outcome of the mass psychology of a large number of ignorant individuals is liable to change violently as a result of a sudden fluctuation of opinion due to factors which do not really make much difference to the prospective yield; since there will be no strong roots of conviction to hold it steady. In abnormal times in particular, when the hypothesis of an indefinite continuance of the existing state of affairs is less plausible than usual even though there are no express grounds to anticipate a definite change, the market will be subject to waves of optimistic and pessimistic sentiment.   (GT, p. 154; see also pp. 153 and 155)

Our conventional assessments remain 'precarious', then (GT, p. 149 and p. 153); for 'the forces of disillusion may suddenly impose a new conventional basis of valuation': there is always the prospect of 'sudden and violent changes', because our judgements of the future have to be 'based on so flimsy a foundation' (thus (f) leads to (g)) (XIV, pp. 114–15). Nor, Keynes contends, are the activities of professional stock market investors likely to exert a stabilising influence, despite the possibility that these are people who might be relatively well-informed; for 'most of these persons are, in fact, largely concerned not with making superior long-term forecasts of the probable yield of an investment over its whole life, but with foreseeing changes in the conventional basis of valuation a short time ahead of the general public' – they are engaged in 'speculation', not 'enterprise', and even 'faith in the conventional basis of valuation having any genuine long-term validity' is not needed for this speculative activity of 'anticipating what average opinion expects the average opinion to be' (GT, pp. 154–8). So Keynes holds it still to be the case that 'the vague panic fears and equally vague and unreasoned hopes are not really lulled, and lie but a little way below the surface' (XIV, p. 155). And he maintains that neglect of this conclusion constitutes a major defect in orthodox theory which, embodying as it does the hypothesis of a calculable future, has led 'to an underestimation of the concealed factors of utter doubt, precariousness, hope and fear' (XIV, p. 122).

There remains the move from (f) combined with (e) to (h) – to the conclusion, that is, that our adoption of merely conventional bases of evaluation, buoyed up by animal spirits, represents a sensible strategy for doing as well as we can in the tight corner uncertainty condemns us to, so that our behaviour can be held to be not unreasonable in the circumstances – circumstances of seriously incomplete information coupled with the necessity to act. Thus Keynes argues, for instance, that:

It would be foolish, in forming our expectations, to attach great weight to matters which are very uncertain. It is reasonable, therefore, to be guided to a considerable degree by the facts about which we feel somewhat confident, even though they may be less decisively relevant to the issue than other facts about which our knowledge is vague and scanty.   (GT, p. 148)

Indeed Keynes judges the convention of taking the present as being a passable guide to the future to be 'a convention of behaviour which none of us could possibly do without' (XIV, p. 125). The link between past experience and future events is of course not logically compelling; but then 'in metaphysics, in science, and in conduct, most of the arguments, upon which we habitually base our rational beliefs, are admitted to be inconclusive in a greater or lesser degree'. But the existence of grounds for doubt, even very serious doubt, does not remove the necessity of acting; and so it is that 'in the actual exercise of reason we do not wait on certainty, or deem it irrational to depend on a doubtful argument' (TP, p. 3).

For Keynes, then, the entrepreneur who surrenders to the urge to activity and refuses to dwell on fears of possible ultimate loss is not acting wantonly but is rather to be likened to 'a healthy man [putting] aside the expectation of death' (GT, p. 162): it would be morbid to allow an insecure future to paralyse rewarding immediate pursuits. Moreover, once organised capital markets exist (and Keynes sees them as fulfilling a useful role in increasing liquidity) then wisdom seems to dictate that the entrepreneur should abide by the conventional, mass valuation of the market, even if he believes himself to have a somewhat superior knowledge of the real prospects of his assets; 'for', writes Keynes;

> there is no sense in building up a new enterprise at a cost greater than that at which a similar existing enterprise can be purchased; whilst there is an inducement to spend on a new project what may seem an extravagant sum, if it can be floated off on the Stock Exchange at an immediate profit.
>
> (GT, p. 151)

Likewise the activity of the professional investor is:

> not the outcome of a wrong-headed propensity. It is an inevitable result of an investment market organised along the lines described. For it is not sensible to pay 25 for an investment of which you believe the prospective yield to justify a value of 30, if you also believe that the market will value it at 20 three months hence. (GT, p. 155)

In this sense, 'the professional investor is forced' by the principles of good sense into his practice of trying 'to guess better than the crowd how the crowd will behave'. He who instead attempts 'investment based on genuine long-term expectation . . . must surely lead much more laborious days and run greater risks . . . and, given equal intelligence, he may make more disastrous mistakes'; and so it is the former 'pastime' which offers 'the higher return . . . to a given stock of intelligence and resources'. And even those 'waves of optimistic and pessimistic sentiment' to which the stock market is subject and which 'are unreasoning' are 'yet in a sense legitimate where no solid basis exists for a reasonable calculation' (GT, pp. 154–7).

There is one passage that encapsulates the theme of the entire argument, with Keynes adding to his (already quoted) claims about the paucity in this context of mathematical expectation an explicit denial that irrational factors then dominate the whole affair:

> We should not conclude from this that everything depends on waves of irrational psychology. On the contrary, the state of long-term expectation is

often steady . . . We are merely reminding ourselves that human decisions affecting the future, whether personal or political or economic, cannot depend on strict mathematical expectation, since the basis for making such calculations does not exist; and that it is our innate urge to activity which makes the wheels go round, our rational selves choosing between the alternatives as best we are able, calculating where we can, but often falling back for our motive on whim or sentiment or chance.   (GT, pp. 162–3)

III

So far, I've given my account of what I believe Keynes' argument about the rationality of our decision procedures under uncertainty to be (section I); and I've tried to show that it's a fair account (section II). This leads up, of course, to the question whether that argument succeeds. How acceptable are its four premises; and are the moves to the remaining propositions sound? I want to approach this question somewhat obliquely, though, because Keynes' treatment of our behaviour in the face of ignorance of the future bears some striking similarities (though the parallel is not complete) to the sceptical view of the philosopher, David Hume; and I'll be suggesting that both Hume's scepticism and subsequent discussions of it, including Keynes' own, have a bearing on the interpretation and the strength of Keynes' position. As a preliminary step, then, this section outlines the correspondence there is between the relevant passages in Hume's philosophy and the various propositions in Keynes' argument.

Some resemblance between Keynes' analysis of actions concerning the future and Hume's work on an allied theme is probably not accidental, for Hume was among those philosophers whom the young Keynes studied deeply and admired. In 1905 when Keynes was just embarking on the study of economics under Marshall and Pigou, he was also busy reading what he called (with justice) 'the superb Hume'[4] and in his first major work – the philosophical *A Treatise on Probability* (1921) – the influence of Hume is strong: he is mentioned in the preface as one of the founders of the 'English' philosophical tradition to which Keynes acknowledges his debt,[5] is frequently referred to in the text, hailed as 'master' of the subject of induction up to that date (TP, p. 304), and is given prominence again on the closing page where Keynes expresses his belief that 'Hume might have read

---

[4] Quoted in Harrod (1951, p. 107).
[5] Scottish Nationalists might cavil at this.

what I have written with sympathy' (TP, p. 468). Then much later in his career Keynes made a lasting contribution to Humean scholarship by – together with Sraffa – identifying a rare and anonymous pamphlet as Hume's work, assembling evidence to clinch its authorship and gaining reprinting for it (Hume's *An Abstract of A Treatise of Human Nature*, reprinted in 1938).[6] Nor was Keynes altogether unusual among economists of his day in his philosophical interest:[7] it would have been reasonable for him to presume some knowledge of philosophy, including an acquaintance with the broad lines of sceptical argument, among his readership for *The General Theory* in the 1930s.

As Keynes puts it in *A Treatise on Probability*, 'Hume showed, not that inductive methods [allowing "inference from past particulars to future generalisations"] were false, but that their validity had never been established and that all possible lines of proof seemed equally unpromising' (TP, p. 302): 'Hume . . . points out that, while it is true that past experience gives rise to a psychological anticipation of some events rather than others, no ground has been given for the validity of this superior anticipation' (TP, p. 88). It is in developing this challenging position that Hume introduces several key propositions that are echoed, I think, in the Keynesian argument:

(1)   Propositions (a), (b) and (c)

Hume is renowned for showing that, when we 'suppose the future conformable to the past . . . however easy this step may seem, reason would never, to all eternity, be able to make it' (AT, p. 16).[8] For, he

---

[6] It was known that such a pamphlet had been written in 1739; but copies were not in general circulation and, moreover, it was supposed that the author had been the young Adam Smith. In their preface to the 'Abstract', Keynes and Sraffa recognise its importance, describing it as 'an introduction to the essence and original genius of the *Treatise*' itself (Hume, 1938, p. xxix).

[7] As the reference to Sraffa above may already have suggested, Harrod (who was an important reader of *The General Theory* at proof stage) was, indeed, a significant philosopher in his own right. So was Frank Ramsey. More generally, the wide significance accorded to philosophy in Keynes' time was evident in the far-reaching influence of Moore and then Wittgenstein at Cambridge: on the former, see O'Donnell (1989); on the latter, see Coates (1990) who argues persuasively that there are some key similarities between the Wittgensteinian revolution in philosophy and Keynes' innovations of method in GT. So I think there was awareness of a broad range of philosophy among Keynes and his fellow economists.

[8] In the references to Hume's writings, the following abbreviations will be used: T for *A Treatise of Human Nature*; AT for *An Abstract of A Treatise of Human Nature*; E for *An Enquiry concerning Human Understanding*; D for *Dialogues concerning Natural Religion*.

writes, 'there can be no *demonstrative* arguments [by which he means, deductions from necessary truths[9]] to prove, that those instances of which we have had no experience, resemble those, of which we have had experience' (T, p. 89). But neither can we arrive at certain knowledge of future events by means merely of deduction from matters of fact (i.e. by arguments which, to the possible confusion of some modern readers, Hume calls 'probable'[10]). For arguments from past experience are themselves 'built on the supposition that there is this conformity betwixt the future and the past, and therefore can never prove it' (AT, p. 15). 'All reasonings from experience', then, depend on 'a step taken by the mind which is not supported by any argument or process of the understanding [in modern terms, by any deductive reasoning]' (E, p. 41; see also E, pp. 33–4, 37–8, 159, 164 and D, p. 87 n. 2). Thus Hume insists on proposition (a) of the structure-diagram above.

Hume also draws a moral about action which, since he does not treat specifically of proposition (b), corresponds to just one element of proposition (c). He writes that if we had to rely on 'reason' (meaning, deduction from the known) alone, 'we should never know how to adjust means to ends, or to employ our natural powers to the production of any effect. There would be an end at once to all action' (E, p. 44).

(2)   Propositions (c), (d) and (e)

Our lack of deductive warrant for inferring the unobserved from the observed does not however lead Hume to say that the activity of forming judgements about the future must therefore be abandoned. On the contrary, he maintains in several statements akin to proposition (d) that there is no choice but to persist: this is 'the whimsical condition of mankind, who must act and reason and believe; though they are not able, by their most diligent enquiry, to satisfy themselves concerning the foundation of these operations, or to remove the objections, which may be raised against them' (E, p. 160). Inference from past experience is 'necessary to the subsistence of our species' (E, p. 55); and in this case as in others nature triumphs over sceptical doubt. This applies even to the sceptic himself, as Hume reports: 'I

[9] See Stove (1965).
[10] When we might still call them demonstrative. On Hume's usage, see Stove (1965 and 1973), who argues that Popper, Flew and others have been misled by it into attributing to Hume an argument about probabilities that he never voiced.

find myself absolutely and necessarily determined to live, and talk, and act like other people in the common affairs of life' (T, p. 269; see also T, pp. 183–4; E, pp. 46, 158, 160; D, p. 9 and p. 87, n. 2). And if indeed we 'cannot subsist' without making inferences from instances of which we have had experience to those as yet unobserved, then (writes Hume) 'if the mind be not engaged by argument to make this step, it must be induced by some other principle of equal weight and authority' (E, p. 41) (see proposition (e)).

(3)   Propositions (e), (f), (g) and (h)

How then *do* our minds make the transition, 'so necessary' in Hume's view, from the observed present to the expected future event? 'Nothing leads us to make this inference' says Hume 'but custom or a certain instinct of our nature' (E, p. 159). 'We are determined by CUSTOM alone to suppose the future conformable to the past' (AT, p. 16). This is surely very like proposition (f). Or again, Hume asserts: 'Custom, then, is the great guide of human life. It is that principle alone which renders our experience useful to us, and makes us expect, for the future, a similar train of events with those which have appeared in the past' (E, p. 44).

Passages such as these, described by Keynes as 'tracing the origin of belief from custom' (AT, p. xxx), complete Hume's main argument on scepticism over induction; but there are also some scattered remarks that could have set Keynes thinking along the lines of the move from proposition (f) to (g) above. In particular, Hume explains how his attitude to sceptical argument is very much a matter of mood: reflecting on the force of sceptical philosophy leads him into a state of 'philosophical melancholy and delirium' which however is soon cured, for a time, by his 'natural propensity, and the course of [his] *animal spirits* and passions'. 'I dine, I play a game of back-gammon, I converse, and am merry with my friends; and when after three or four hours' amusement, I would return to these speculations, they appear so cold, and strained, and ridiculous, that I cannot find in my heart to enter into them any farther' (T, pp. 268–71, my emphasis). All the same, just as the 'vague panic fears' that Keynes detects beneath the smooth veneer of the investment market 'are not really lulled', so also 'sceptical doubt' in Hume's view 'can never be radically cured, but must return upon us every moment, however we may chase it away, and sometimes may seem entirely free from it . . . Carelessness and inattention alone can afford us any remedy' (T, p. 218; see also D, p. 7).

Does Hume nevertheless think we have good reasons for forging ahead with our activities, using past experience as our guide despite this unsquashable doubt? Would he be likely to accept proposition (h)? This is controversial: there is evidence on both sides (although maintaining Hume's opposition to (h) would be more orthodox[11]). Here I merely note as casual evidence for the *un*orthodox position Hume's remark that 'for [his] conduct' (acting, living and so on) the sceptic 'is not obliged to give any other reason than the absolute necessity he lies under of doing so' (D, p. 9); his suggestion that the natural, instinctive force of habit or custom may have some advantages over the working of deductive reasoning, being able to operate strongly, for instance, in 'the first years of infancy' (E, p. 55: see also T, p. 187); his willingness to allow that an anticipated effect may '*justly* be inferred' from the observation in the relevant circumstances of what has hitherto appeared as a cause (E, p. 34, my emphasis; and see T, p. 124); and lastly his admission that, be sceptical objections what they may, 'none but *a fool or a madman* will ever pretend to dispute the authority of experience, or to reject that great guide of human life' (E, p. 36, my emphasis again).

It is Hume's general matter of fact approach that Keynes seems most to have admired in his philosophy, identifying him with 'common sense and a sort of hard-headed practicality towards the whole business' (X, p. 339; see also TP, preface). 'He stands', says Keynes, 'for the plain man against the sophisms and ingenuities of metaphysicians, logicians, mathematicians and even theologians' (TP, p. 56). Of course Keynes' commitment to (h) is clearer: he *certainly* did not believe that we must rest content with truly extreme sceptical conclusions. But the extent of the parallel just described between his argument and Hume's shows, I think, that in his economic work it is at least the case that, as Harrod suggested for philosophy, 'Keynes took Hume's scepticism seriously' (Harrod, 1951, p. 656).

IV

It's now time to consider how successful the argument set out in section I is.

[11] See for instance, Stove (1973, p. 50), and Popkin (1951). Keynes himself tends to interpret Hume in a fairly orthodox way.

First, what of the four premises: propositions (a), (b), (d) and (f)? I think there is good reason to accept them but that each of the first three needs some further explanation. Proposition (f) will simply be taken to be (what Keynes persuasively presents it as) a correct statement of fact about our conventional method of selecting actions in practice,[12] with which – it will also be assumed – proposition (g) (scope for irrational influences) is legitimately associated.

Proposition (d) (necessity of action, etc.) generates more doubt: for, after all, a prolonged period of inaction does not seem inconceivable – is deciding not to act still to count as a form of action? But here Hume's argument, with its reference to that which is 'necessary to the subsistence of our species', suggests what is intended: such a period must yield to one of positive action in the *end* – if human agents are to survive. Grant then that survival requires action in the end: does it also require investment? Keynes needs this to be so for the specific form of his argument and I think it a pity that he does not justify it more explicitly. However, there does seem to be truth in what I take to be Keynes' point – that rather similarly investment is imperative for the *community* in the sense that it is necessary if the system of production is to survive for future generations.[13]

Proposition (a) (no proof possible for the future course of events, etc.) seems plain sailing in the light of the backing Hume supplies for it. (Here I'm taking it, of course, that when Keynes writes 'we do not know what the future holds', he means, like Hume, that we don't attain *deductive* certainty.) Section III showed Hume making two powerful points against the claim that the character of future events *can* be deduced from past experience: first, that this isn't a necessary truth; and second, that it can't itself be deduced from past experience without circularity. Because of their vividness, let me add here two

---

[12] Modern work on induction also gives convention a significant role, 'well-entrenched' predicates (such as 'green') being readily projected into the future, poorly entrenched ones (such as 'grue') not (see Goodman, 1954). And Heiner (1983) discusses the significance for economics of rules of thumb.

It is in this connection that Keynes appeals to his treatment in TP of the importance of considering 'the *weight* of arguments': there is a high weight of evidence about the present and recent past, and this is one factor, Keynes suggests, that helps to create confidence in practice in our (still vulnerable) convention of projecting existing trends into the future (GT, p. 148; TP, chapter 6; compare also GT, p. 240). On weight, see Runde (1990).

[13] The necessity argument would be considerably less strong for the *individual* entrepreneur: see Matthews (essay 7) in this volume.

passages from Russell that amplify these Humean moves. Here's the first:

> We are all convinced that the sun will rise tomorrow. Why? . . . We have a firm belief that it will rise in the future, because it has risen in the past . . . [However] we know that . . . expectations of uniformity are liable to be misleading. The man who has fed the chicken every day throughout its life at last wrings its neck instead . . . Thus our instincts certainly cause us to believe that the sun will rise tomorrow, but we may be in no better a position than the chicken which unexpectedly has its neck wrung.

Thus it is always logically possible that physical regularities of the past will collapse in the future. And (here's the second) there is no escape via the argument that, for uniformities to which there are no known exceptions, we know that 'the future will resemble the past, because what was the future has constantly become the past, and has always been found to resemble the past, so that we really have experience of the future, namely of times which were formerly future, which we may call past futures'. For such an argument 'really begs the very question at issue. We have experience of past futures, but not of future futures, and the question is: Will future futures resemble past futures?' (Russell 1912, pp. 33–6).[14] As Hume maintained, then, 'all reasonings from experience' ultimately depend on a non-deductive step; and proposition (a) is home and dry.

Proposition (b) has a less secure passage, however. A natural response to proposition (a) is to suggest that, though we are not able to reach certain knowledge of future events just by means of *de*duction, nevertheless *in*duction from past experience may sometimes permit us to judge them probable; and in fact both Keynes and Russell do respond in this way.[15] But Keynes still maintains that our information is generally too thin to enable the mathematical calculus of probabilities to be used to determine our rational course of action, for he holds it to be far from universally the case that degrees of

---

[14] Russell applies this argument not just to statements of regularity but also to what are regarded as laws.

On resemblance between past and future, Keynes' wording is surely incautious in the Galton Lecture when he writes that 'the future never resembles the past' and that it is 'contrary to all likelihood' that it will do so (XIV, p. 124): passages elsewhere suggest he means simply that the future situation facing us never *precisely* resembles the past (there typically being, indeed, marked changes over any considerable interval of time).

[15] Russell's *The Problems of Philosophy* giving publicity to Keynes' ideas of probability, says Braithwaite in his Foreword to TP.

probability are measurable as he claims the orthodox approach requires. Why?

The grounds Keynes could give for proposition (b) are supplied in his *Treatise on Probability*. In his view, 'the theory of probability is logical . . . because it is concerned with the degree of belief which it is *rational* to entertain in given conditions, and not merely with the actual beliefs of particular individuals, which may or may not be rational' (TP, p. 4).[16] But often the rational degree of belief will not be precise: one of Keynes' main theses in the first part of this book is that it is only 'in a very special type of case' that 'a meaning can be given to a *numerical* comparison of magnitude' between probabilities (TP, pp. 36–7), whilst 'there are . . . many cases in which . . . the probabilities are, in fact, *not comparable*' at all (TP, p. 122).[17]

Keynes supports his conclusion about the limitations on our ability to measure probabilities with the suggestion that probability statements express a relation (between premises and conclusion) which is analogous in respect of measurement to the relation of similarity: for

[16] But the rational probability judgements Keynes is concerned with are, however, also specific to the individual: he aims to exclude from his enquiry believing something probable 'for a reason which is preposterous or for no reason at all' (TP, p. 10) but to admit judgements which, though not supported by the full evidence, yet appear to the judger to be supported by the evidence available to him at the time. (Keynes also allows that not only knowledge but also 'powers', the 'constitution' of the mind, may vary from person to person and so acknowledges another element that is 'subjective in the sense of being relative to the individual' (TP, pp. 18 19), although 'in the sense important to logic, probability is not subjective . . . not . . . subject to human caprice' (TP, p. 4).)

[17] In Luce and Raiffa's (1957) terminology, the calculus of 'risk' can be brought into play in a decision problem in which the consequences of possible actions are not known with certainty, provided the decider attaches – *no matter how* – a numerical probability to each of the possible outcomes of the different actions open to him; whilst if he doesn't attach such probabilities to the outcomes, he is said to make his decision 'under uncertainty' (see Bacharach, 1976, p. 14). Keynes clearly argues that subjective probabilities, rationally (reasonably) assigned, are typically not numerically measurable; but would he also hold that the decision-maker is typically bereft even of an arbitrary numerical assignment in his mind? I fancy he would (and differ here from Minsky's interpretation; see Minsky, 1975, p. 65); so that, on his analysis economic agents typically make decisions 'under uncertainty' (see also Champernowne, 1969, pp. 10–11, 76, 96) – whereas neoclassical analysis concentrates in effect on risk.

Keynes' position contrasts with the Bayesian approach brought into prominence by Jeffreys' *Theory of Probability*. But the justification Jeffreys offers in his *Scientific Inference* (1931) for assuming that all probabilities *can* be expressed by numbers does not seem a convincing answer to Keynes, amounting to little more than the claim that such an assumption makes the subject more tractable: 'my real objection to Keynes' [position] is that it is one of those attempts at generality that in practice lead only to vagueness' (p. 223).

both, precise quantitative measurements are rarely on the cards; yet ordinal comparisons *can* sometimes be made – but only in a restricted set of cases.[18] There is more to his argument (for the full story, see TP, especially Part I, chapter 3); but its character perhaps emerges well enough from some of the illustrations he gives of cases in which assessment of probability is tricky or impossible. For instance, he contends that only ordinal ranking of probability is possible in the following common case: 'Consider an induction or a generalisation. It is usually held that each additional instance increases the generalisation's probability . . . [But] there is no basis for an estimate *how much* stronger or weaker the new argument is than the old' (TP, pp. 30–1). Thus:

We know that the probability of a well-established induction is great, but, when we are asked to name its degree, we cannot. Common sense tells us that some inductive arguments are stronger than others, and that some are very strong. But how much stronger or how strong we cannot express. The probability of an induction is only numerically definite when we are able to

[18] Ordinal comparisons of probability not uncommonly being possible among a set of propositions concerned with the same subject-matter but only exceptionally between them and members of a set dealing with something else. Keynes illustrates his argument that only a partial ordering of probabilities is possible with the diagram below (TP, p. 42), in which numerical probabilities lie along the line OAI, points along OVWXI can be compared ordinally (similarly for OZWYI and OUI), Y and V are unusual in being ordinally comparable by means of a common reference point, W (similarly for X and Z) but no comparison is possible between U, Z and V (or U, X and Y).

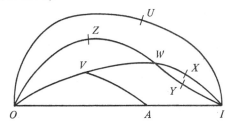

There seems to be some truth in the analogy with similarity – try: 'New York looks more like Rio than like the rain forest' and 'Ex-President Nixon is more likely to detest tape recordings than Yehudi Menuhin is'. Jeffreys however simply brushes aside the whole approach, dismissing the spatial comparisons suggested by the diagram: 'Keynes' alternative [to the Jeffreys theory] is something like the view that probabilities resemble places on the earth's surface; we might say that New York and London are both between the North and South Poles but neither New York or London is between the other and the North Pole. It seems to me that all probabilities actually are comparable and that Keynes is merely creating difficulties' (Jeffreys, 1931, p. 223).

make definite assumptions about the number of independent equiprobable influences at work.   (TP, p. 288)[19]

But in many other cases even ordinal ranking cannot be carried out:

Consider three sets of experiments, each directed towards establishing a generalisation. The first set is more numerous; in the second set the irrelevant conditions have been more carefully varied; in the third case the generalisation in view is wider in scope than the others. Which of these generalisations is on such evidence the most probable? There is, surely, no answer; there is neither equality nor inequality between them . . . If the grounds in the . . . cases are quite different, even a comparison of more or less, let alone numerical measurement, may be impossible.   (TP, pp. 31–2)

Nor is it even possible:

[to] say in the case of every argument whether it is *more* or *less* likely than not. Is our expectation of rain, when we start out for a walk, always *more* likely than not, or *less* likely than not, or *as* likely as not? I am prepared to argue that on some occasions *none* of these alternatives hold . . . .If the barometer is high, but the clouds are black, it is not always rational that one should prevail over the other in our minds, or even that we should balance them.

(TP, p. 32)

In sum, then, 'a numerical measure of degrees of probability . . . is only occasionally possible. A rule can be given for numerical measurement when the conclusion is one of a number of equiprobable, exclusive alternatives [as in throwing a die], but not otherwise' (TP, p. 122).

All this makes rather clearer, I think, Keynes' meaning in his QJE article of 1937 when he compares the expectation of the rate of interest in twenty years time or that of the obsolescence of a new invention with the expectation of a Victory bond being drawn. The latter case is one merely of risk because it fulfils the conditions under which numerical measurement of probability can be achieved; whereas the former pair are regarded by Keynes as cases of complete

[19] Keynes argues that such difficulties are aggravated when our experience is only of a frequent, instead of an unfailing, association. He writes: 'Nobody supposes that we can measure exactly the probability of an induction. Yet many persons seem to believe that in the weaker and much more difficult type of argument, where the association under our examination has been in our experience, not invariable, but merely in a certain proportion, we can attribute a definite measure to our future expectations and can claim practical certainty for the results of predictions which lie within relatively narrow limits. Coolly considered, this is a preposterous claim, which would have been universally rejected long ago, if those who made it had not so successfully concealed themselves from the eyes of common sense in a maze of mathematics' (TP, p. 424).

uncertainty since in them no rational comparison of magnitude between the probabilities of various possible outcomes is possible: our basis for prediction in them may be no better than that in the situation in which the auspicious barometer reading combines with a threatening sky – either (as in that case) the various snippets of information can't be reconciled or compared, or relevant information simply isn't available.[20]

In the *Treatise on Probability* (pp. 343–9), Keynes uses these claims about the narrow scope for numerical measures of probability in an argument that is a precursor of *The General Theory's* when he launches an attack on the Benthamite thesis about 'what ought to be our preference in regard to various alternative courses of action'; and this early version is helpfully explicit on the link between propositions (b) and (c). Keynes' claim is that the Benthamite calculus *relies* on the assumption 'that degrees of probability . . . are numerically measurable' and are 'wholly subject to the laws of arithmetic' (an assumption which of course 'runs directly counter' to Keynes' view). And this is because, if choice between various courses of action is to be made in familiar fashion by summing for each of them a series of terms made up of the mathematical expectations (possible gain times 'probability of attaining it') of each possible consequence so as to select the action with the highest sum, it is only if probability is numerically measurable that such a procedure will always yield a determinate solution.[21] For even if *ordinal* measurement of probability were

---

[20] There are intermediate cases (such as well-established universal inductions or inductive correlations) in which the probabilities involved lend themselves to some comparisons of magnitude but fall short of exact numerical measurement – cases of uncertainty, then, in the technical sense, but not of, so to speak, gross uncertainty. Thus in the same passage Keynes writes of the weather as 'only moderately uncertain' and the expectation of life as 'only slightly uncertain'. And in these two cases, in contrast with the examples of long-term investments, there is also a reasonable weight of relevant and cumulative evidence to draw on, so that probability judgements can in practice be made with a modest degree of confidence (see TP, pp. 81–3), leaving less 'uncertainty' in the psychological sense too (see TP, p. 15).

[21] And *then* only if, also, the possible gains (utilities) are similarly 'subject to the laws of arithmetic' whilst risk-aversion and the 'weights' of the arguments can be ignored. Keynes emphasises that even if all the difficulties over numerical measurement were waived, still: 'the doctrine that the "mathematical expectations" of alternative courses of action are the proper measures of our degrees of preference is open to doubt on two grounds – first because it ignores what [may be] termed . . . the "weights" of the arguments, namely, the amount of evidence upon which each probabilities is founded; and second, because it ignores the element of "risk" and assumes that an even chance of heaven or hell is precisely as much to be desired as the certain attainment of a state of mediocrity' (TP, p. 344; but compare too pp. 81–3).

always possible – and of course, reinforcing the point, Keynes contends that it is *not* – still this wouldn't suffice to ensure comparability between the mathematical expectations themselves or between their sums. This is why he slates the Benthamite blueprint for decision-making as a 'pseudo-rationalistic' theory that 'no one has ever acted on', involving 'a mythical system of probable knowledge' (XIV, p. 124); and it is why he sees his conclusion that degrees of probability are numerically measurable 'only in a strictly limited class of cases' as being so damaging for the orthodox treatment of 'human decisions affecting the future'.

But the approach of *A Treatise on Probability* has not commanded by any means universal assent; and this element in Keynes' argument is relatively vulnerable to orthodox attack. It lacks the conclusive backing available to proposition (a); and, though Keynes does present an appealing *prima facie* case for it, proposition (b) is to be entered as a premise with some hesitation.

Suppose, however, that we accept the four premises now discussed ((a), (b), (d) and (f)), at least provisionally. How does the rest of the argument fare? All but one of the steps in it (the moves to propositions (c), (e) and (g)) seem relatively straightforward.

The remaining – considerable – difficulties then centre on the derivation of proposition (h) (decision procedures not unreasonable in the circumstances). One immediate problem is posed by the absence of general agreement over the meaning of 'reasonable' and 'unreasonable', 'rational' and 'irrational'. So far as Keynes' own usage goes, it appears from his *Treatise on Probability* that he tends to treat 'reasonable' and 'rational' as equivalent (see, e.g. TP, pp. 246, 272–5) and looks on actions as being rational if they are justified in the light of the agent's rational beliefs, where these are the beliefs it is reasonable (sensible) for the agent to form given the information available to him at the relevant time but which of course, in spite of his good reasons for holding them, will by no means necessarily turn out to be true (see TP, pp. 339, 272–5, 10–11). Acts which are rational in this, fairly broad, sense might well be judged mistaken in retrospect, then; but yet Keynes avoids the pitfall of defining 'rational' in such a way that no action could count as irrational.[22] He also allows that rational action doesn't automatically require con-

---

[22] A trap I think von Mises (1981, pp. 32–3) does fall into. On Keynes' avoidance of it, see also n. 16 above.

scious deliberation at the time, sometimes involving instead, for instance, reliance on 'unconscious memory', a 'habit' of the mind (TP, p. 15). His general understanding of the rationality concept would, I think, find a fair measure of support within philosophy:[23] the idea about habit, for example, gains backing from Hollis, who writes:

> to insist on conscious deliberation is to miss the place of habit in rational action. The rational way to drive a car is precisely not to deliberate each change of gear but to master the skill so well that no deliberation is needed. There are rational habits and, were there not, we could not talk, plan, associate, build, reason or perform many other tasks which make social life possible. Rational action is a skill requiring habit and, if the point is missed, large areas of social action are wrongly classed as non-rational, with great harm to the social sciences. (Hollis 1977, p. 17)

However orthodox economic theory has typically used the word 'rational' in a very much narrower sense than Keynes. Its standard practice has been to identify rationality with 'substantive rationality' (as Simon puts it), with action, that is, that (for given goals) does achieve the objectively best solution. Thus there has been a tradition of identifying the rational with the ideal. Shackle goes so far as to write that orthodox theory has assumed 'perfect rationality' and regarded rationality as perfect 'only . . . when relevant knowledge is perfect' (Shackle 1967, p. 295).[24] It is conceivable that Shackle is using the word in this extremely narrow sense himself when he presents the essence of Keynes' theory as being that 'rational expectation being unattainable, we substitute for it first one and then another kind of irrational expectation' (Shackle, p. 129), or again when he writes that 'the message of the *General Theory*' is that 'investment is an *irrational* activity, or a non-rational one' (Shackle, p. 130) – claims that, on the face of it, clash with the interpretation of Keynes' analysis as culminating in proposition (h) but that *could* just amount, if Shackle is echoing but not endorsing traditional economic usage, to the safe contention that Keynes' theory of investment is not one of *substantive*

---

[23] See, e.g. Raz (1975).

Proposition (h) describes our decision-making as 'not unreasonable'. This could be regarded as less strong than calling it 'reasonable' – though Keynes in places seems willing to make the latter claim too.

[24] It seems likely that Keynes would have felt that the 'rational expectations' hypothesis, with its somewhat *less* exacting requirements, still sets the standard for rationality unreasonably high. (Again, modern orthodox notions of rationality that focus on consistency and expected (not realised) utility would be somewhat less strict than Shackle's version.)

rationality. It could still be rational in Keynes' wide sense to do what would count as irrational on the narrower definition. But this is then another point at which orthodox economists might be inclined to quarrel with Keynes' argument. Plainly acceptance of proposition (h) depends partly on willingness to use 'rational' and 'reasonable' in a comparatively broad way – a way that can however, I think, be judged reasonable itself.[25]

But though taking 'rational' in a wide sense is necessary for the success of Keynes' conclusion, it isn't sufficient. Once purely conventional procedures (proposition (f)) and psychological influences (proposition (g)) are admitted as key components of decision-making, it might be thought that reason, however generally defined, *has* been abandoned. Shackle at times seems to suppose that Keynes himself thought this: he gives an interpretation that clearly does conflict with mine when he writes of 'the nihilism of Keynes' final position' (1967, p. 247).[26] As section II showed, Keynes was not in fact so negative. But should he have been, given the rest of his argument? What ground is there for believing that, in adopting the various mere conventions Keynes outlines – especially that of assuming that the future will resemble the past – we *are* following a sensible strategy in the circumstances?

It is now that Keynes' intertwining of his case about investment with his general argument about future-regarding decisions becomes seriously confusing. For it seems that in the general case what is chiefly at issue is simply the classic philosophical question whether inductive procedures – linking the unobserved with the observed – can be justified. And yet there must be much more to the specific investment case than this: after all, for practical purposes, we need not generally trouble ourselves over the sceptical doubt about induction that infects even the securest inductive conclusions (such as that the sun will rise again tomorrow); whereas the doubt Keynes seems to stress in the context of investment decisions is typically far more immediate – the *pressing* doubt that arises because there may be only

---

[25] Think of the common cases (stressed by J.S. Mill) in which, because time is strictly limited, it is reasonable to abide by simple rules of thumb, that yield a good but less than perfect result. (See GT, p. 51; Raz, 1975, pp. 59–61; and Simon, 1976, esp. section 2, 'Procedural Rationality'.) No doubt Keynes would have been sympathetic to the procedural rationality concept which Simon opposes to the substantive notion.

[26] Or again, of Keynes regarding expectations of future asset values as mere 'figments of imaginative thought' (Shackle, 1967, p. 246).

the flimsiest evidence to support one conclusion rather than another, so that there is pitifully little for inductive procedures themselves to go on. The reasonableness of general inductive method, then (supposing this could be shown) wouldn't automatically carry over to the apparently similar conventional procedures that Keynes describes for investment. But still the resolution of the question whether inductive reasoning can be defended is a highly significant element in Keynes' attitude to rational decisions about the future and it is convenient to take his approach to this first.

Not surprisingly this issue has been hotly debated in philosophy ever since Hume's demonstration that the move to an inductive conclusion is not one that reason 'determines' us to make, meaning by 'reason' (as was usual at that time) just deductive reasoning. Hume's wording of his argument may have fostered the tendency which still exists in social science to identify reason and rationality with the process of deduction, rationality then having to bear a narrow sense. But it was not Hume's intention to suggest that deductive reasoning constitutes the sole standard by which mental activity should be judged: indeed he held that deductive reasoning, like induction, was itself open to sceptical challenge. Section III suggested that there is room for some debate over how extreme Hume's own scepticism is, but that *some* case might be made out for interpreting him as saying that our making inferences by means of the mere inductive 'habit of the mind' – by means, that is, merely of 'custom' – isn't foolish (and thus isn't unreasonable or irrational in Keynes' sense); and one argument from the literature discussing Hume's position seems relevant to the assessment of proposition (h). According to Hume, when we draw a well-grounded inductive conclusion nature presents us with no viable option. But the very fact that we are merely making Hobson's choice may amount to some defence of our procedure, giving an argument against its censure as unreasonable or daft. Thus Lenz has maintained that if we 'cannot avoid making' such inferences 'any injunction not to do so is beside the point' (Lenz 1958, p. 183).[27] And this could be enough at least to rule out the claim that the inductive method is unreasonable, if that claim always goes along with an implicit instruction to abandon it. Keynes might well agree with this justification, so far as it goes:

---

[27] Lenz (1958 – who was writing specifically about Hume's account of causal inference) points out that the 'natural' or 'unavoidable' character of inductive inferences is *not* shared by all beliefs.

certainly he seems to share Hume's view that the inductive convention of assuming past regularities will persist is in some way forced on us – 'a convention of behaviour which none of us could possibly do without' – and he writes of the way in which 'the inductive method' is embedded in 'the organon of thought' (TP, p. 294). But in fact he argues for more full-blooded defence of inductive reasoning than stems just from maintaining its unavoidability.

Whilst Keynes did accept the sceptical argument that 'almost all our beliefs in matters of experience, undoubtedly depend on a strong psychological propensity in us to consider objects in a particular light', he also held that unless this conclusion is qualified 'such scepticism goes too far', arguing that the dependence of these beliefs on the psychological process of habitual association 'is no ground for supposing that they are nothing more than "lively imaginations" . . . we may believe that our judgements can penetrate into the real world, even though their credentials are subjective' (TP, p. 56). In the *Treatise on Probability*, he attempted to justify inductive reasoning by appeal to a hypothesis of 'the limitation of independent variety' – though he did not finally succeed in offering any better basis for that hypothesis than simply its being a 'valid principle darkly present to our minds' (TP, chapter 22). Later, responding to Ramsey's criticism of this thesis, Keynes allowed instead that the basis of such reasoning 'is part of our human outfit, perhaps given us merely by natural selection'. But he still felt there was more to be said, writing that 'it is not getting to the bottom of the principle of induction merely to say that it is a useful mental habit' (X, p. 339).[28]

Perhaps he would have greeted with enthusiasm the rather persuasive answer given more recently, by Strawson, to the question whether our habit of forming inductive expectations can be rationally justified. Strawson contends that the statement 'induction is rational (reasonable)' is not only true but is a *necessary* truth. He argues that 'the rationality of induction . . . is a matter of what we mean by the word "rational" on its application to any procedure for forming opinions about what lies outside our observations or that of available witnesses. For to have good reasons for any such opinion *is* to have good inductive support for it' (Strawson 1952, pp. 261–2, my emphasis). On such an approach, following our well-established inductive procedures is rational or reasonable, conventional though

[28] Though see Goodman (1954).

they be. And it clearly is Keynes' view that argument by induction *does* lead to knowledge of the future *of a sort*: to less-than-certain knowledge which Keynes calls 'probable'.[29] He suggests that philosophy has in the main been too preoccupied with the pursuit of demonstrative certainty (TP, p. 266), tending to neglect 'the study of arguments, to which it is rational to attach *some* weight' but which are (by deductive standards) inconclusive – despite the fact that the neglected group includes a limited set of inductive conclusions of which, though we cannot precisely measure their probability, yet 'we are very well assured' and 'upon which it is rational to act with the utmost confidence' (TP, p. 275).

This explains, I think, a number of the remarks of Keynes quoted in section II which would otherwise seem anomalous. For although he surely does maintain that 'we do not know what the future holds', yet at other times he might appear to be weakening this when he speaks merely of 'the future about which we know so *little*' (XIV, p. 121, my emphasis; and similarly, XIV, p. 124; GT, pp. 149, 150) and of our having '*as a rule*, only the vaguest idea of any *but the most direct consequences of our acts*' (XIV, p. 113, my emphasis). The puzzle is persistent; for again, our convention is, he says, to assume indefinite continuance of the existing state of affairs 'except insofar as we have specific reasons to expect a change' (GT, p. 152; and similarly, GT, pp. 148, 154; XIV, p. 114): yet if we can know nothing at all of the future, how can we have grounds for expecting a specific change? By inductive reasoning, is of course the answer – reasoning which Keynes believes to be justified as rational or reasonable and which he sees as providing some (almost always non-numerical) 'probable knowledge' of what is to come, even though it remains true that we know nothing with deductive certainty about the future. Suppose the environment has been uniform in some respects over a period of time. Then 'we cannot be sure that such conditions will persist', says Keynes, continuing however: 'But if we find them in the past, we have at any rate some basis for an inductive argument' (XIV, p. 316). That inductive reasoning to 'probable' knowledge is what Keynes has in mind in the puzzling passages is further confirmed by some specific examples he gives of cases in which he judges expectations of the future to be comparatively secure. One is that of

---

[29] His use of the term 'probable' is of course very broad and differs from that of some philosophers.

the producer who just has to form short-term expectations: it is 'sensible' for him to assume that 'the most recently realised results will continue, except in so far as there are definite reasons for expecting a change' because, Keynes maintains, 'a large part of the circumstances usually continue unchanged from one day to the next' (GT, p. 51): there are *good in*ductive grounds for projecting present results in this fairly stable immediate environment. Or again, to take a case involving inductive grounds for predicting change, it was 'known' in 1937 'much more securely than we know almost any other social or economic factor relating to the future' that there would shortly be a 'change-over' in the trend of population (from rising to stationary or declining), this 'unusual degree of knowledge concerning the future' resulting from the 'time-lag in the effects of vital statistics' (XIV, p. 125). It will perhaps be rare for inductive procedures to yield conclusions of which we feel thoroughly assured. But once the convention of assuming continuity is accepted, past evidence will frequently support *some* (sometimes considerable) degree of belief in propositions about the future – especially about the *near* future, Keynes believes.[30] It is in this way according to Keynes that we may rationally form the 'best expectations' we can, on which we may often act with some degree of confidence but which are typically much too imprecise to furnish material for nice Benthamite techniques of calculation, and which of course never in principle escape the risk of 'failure at the last, as in the case of the chicken whose neck is wrung' (Russell, p. 36).

All this relates to the general method of making decisions about the future. But there is still a large question about the investment decision; for it does seem surprising that Keynes should so stress the role of our conventional assumption that future events will be like those already observed in the context of long-term economic expectation in which, as he also emphasises, *gross* uncertainty is often paramount. Doesn't he seem to suggest that, in investing, we are typically concerned with the remoter consequences of our acts (XIV, p. 113) and then won't even judgements of the more and the less probable tend to be beyond us? Won't induction be virtually powerless here?

Yet once more there are conflicting statements. 'We simply do not

---

[30] He argues in TP (pp. 287–8) that belief in the greater security of inductive reasoning concerned only with a single event in the immediate future needn't be arbitrary.

know' when a new invention will become obsolete or what the rate of interest will be twenty years from now (XIV, pp. 113–14). On the other hand, the entrepreneur is supposed by Keynes to enjoy an 'element of real knowledge' (based on 'special knowledge of the circumstances, either actual or prospective, of the business in question') about the value of investment he undertakes, that element which is reduced once ownership and management become divorced (GT, p. 153). And again, Keynes holds it to be possible that the professional investor on the stock market may also possess 'judgement and knowledge beyond that of the average private investor' (GT, p. 154); and investment based on 'genuine long-term expectation' is held to be 'socially advantageous' and, though laborious, risky and even 'scarcely practicable', yet not totally out of the question (GT, p. 157). Moreover, Keynes explicitly allows at the end of chapter 12 of *The General Theory* that 'there are . . . certain important factors which somewhat mitigate in practice the effects of our ignorance of the future' – amongst them 'the operation of compound interest combined with the likelihood of obsolescence with the passage of time', because of which the prospective yield for many individual investments 'is legitimately dominated by the returns of the comparatively near future' (GT, p. 163),[31] the immediate future setting a time-horizon over which the supposition of the future being like the past is more likely to come near the mark in his view, making projection of key features of the existing situation an acceptable rule of thumb. It seems fairly plain that Keynes does not after all mean to maintain that in the nature of things *all* investment has to be made under conditions of such complete uncertainty that inductive reasoning about future profit flows could not get any grip.

This tends to help proposition (h) but might be thought to jeopardise the excitement of Keynes' argument. If his essential point were to turn out after all to be that investment plans are made on the basis of induction rather than (as in orthodoxy) deduction, one might be left wondering whether lack of certainty of that sort merited *quite* such a fuss, and feeling that proposition (g) (fragility of conventions

---

[31] The examples of investment in buildings (where special benefits to occupiers may be set against the risk), in public utilities (where to a greater extent than elsewhere, the future yield can be predetermined by human intervention), and by public authorities (where prospective social advantage may weigh more strongly than questions of expected monetary yield) are given too.

allowing panic, hysteria, sudden collapse and so on) was exaggerated. But in fact there are two reasons why extreme uncertainty does still lie at the centre of Keynes' account of investment decisions. The first and perhaps more important is that it is the 'average private investor' on the stock market who in fact sets the pattern for others (see section II). And he *is* without 'special knowledge of the circumstances' of the businesses in some of which he means to invest. So in forming his expectations of their long-term prospects, he is not able to reason inductively that, say, one company or another has rosy prospects if current evidence is projected forwards. His existing knowledge of the firms in question is typically restricted largely to the stock market's recent valuation of them; and it is just this that, acting on the usual convention, he projects into the future. Yet Keynes contends that observation of the market over a period of time doesn't justify great reliance on the permanence of its existing valuations: he writes that 'the actual results of [such] an investment over a long term of years very seldom agree with the initial expectation'. In this standard case, then, we do not 'really believe' in our conventional assumption 'that the existing state of affairs will continue indefinitely. [Indeed] we know from extensive experience that this is most unlikely' (GT, p. 152). The second reason relates to firms' internally financed investment in real productive assets: it is that there will still remain *some* cases in which distant prospects dominate and the 'mitigating' factors have little effect. For example, with a very long-term investment project, there may be no pay-off in the early years; and the extent to which there'll be one in the end may depend on matters on which no clear 'special knowledge' is at present to be had, even by the entrepreneur – on 'the prospect of a European war', 'the price of copper . . . twenty years hence' or the like, factors for which there is no adequate inductive basis for prediction and about which indeed 'we simply do not know'. Gross uncertainty reinstated then; but questions about the wisdom of our response to it also renewed.

Consider first the financial investors' usual decision procedure which takes existing valuations as a reliable guide, in spite of their long-run unreliability. Can this be judged reasonable? Keynes' suggestion is that it can, on the grounds that general action in accordance with this convention *itself affects the market*, contributing to the (largely market-determined) security of investment of this kind. The 'conventional method of calculation will be compatible with a considerable measure of continuity and stability in our affairs', he explains, '*so long as we can rely on the maintenance of the convention*' (GT, p. 152). In these circumstances, the investor (who is of course able to sell his shares again at comparatively short notice) 'can legitimately encourage himself with the idea that the only risk he runs is that of a genuine change in the news *over the near future*, as to the likelihood of which he can attempt to form his own judgement, and which is unlikely to be very large'; and 'he need not lose his sleep merely because he has not any notion what his investment will be worth ten years hence' (GT, pp. 152–3). If such a form of behaviour is conventional, then, so that others will typically adopt it too, the problem of selecting investments on the stock-market reduces to what Keynes sees as the more tractable one of foreseeing changes only a little time ahead. In this way, though the system is inherently fragile, still 'investment becomes reasonably "safe" for the individual investor over short periods' (GT, p. 153); and accordingly his routine assessment of the prospects *is* judged to be a sensible one.

However, the claim that it isn't silly to rely on the convention of projecting existing trends does seem more at risk in the case of the entrepreneur making long-term investments in physical assets with a long gestation period. Granted that in our ignorance 'we must be guided by some hypothesis', the question arises acutely here: why by *this* one? Adopting it scarcely seems 'unavoidable' now: for instance, not having the foggiest idea what it would be best to do, mightn't believers pray for guidance and non-believers reasonably simply toss a coin? I suppose Keynes *might* reply that an answered prayer changes the situation to one of knowledge: routine behaviour could still be reasonable so long as the circumstance of ignorance remains. And he hints at what his answer to the coin-tossing option might be – that tossing a coin would at least have no *advantage* over a habitual response; for he argues that a state of ignorance is not an adequate basis in itself for assigning equiprobabilities to gain and loss (GT, p. 152; TP, chapter 4).[32] He might also think (I speculate because he fails to spell out his case, though explicitness was surely needed) that since we adopt the usual convention in other types of investment decision, it may naturally occur to us here too and perhaps may serve the purpose as well as any other method (our confidence in it, however, very probably remaining especially weak (see GT, p. 148) and markedly needing the boost of 'animal spirits'). It seems that it may be on some such grounds as these that Keynes judges to be not

---

[32] Again in contrast with Jeffreys' approach (see Jeffreys, 1948, chapter 1, section 4).

*un*reasonable our way of handling this group of particularly intractable investment decisions. This is further suggested by his view of how we ought to act in another situation of complete uncertainty – the perplexing conjunction of the encouraging barometer reading with the darkened sky. The expectation of rain then being, as he reasons, neither more nor less nor as likely as not, 'it will be an arbitrary matter to decide for or against the umbrella' and, furthermore, 'it will be *rational* to allow caprice to determine us [carry it if you usually do?] and to waste no time on the debate' (TP, p. 32, my emphasis).

These then are the many (though mixed and occasionally muddling) grounds Keynes seems to have or to hint at for holding that proposition (h) applies both to our general methods of decision about the future and to our procedures for making investment decisions of various kinds.

This completes the account of the strengths and weaknesses of Keynes' argument. It is a complex argument, sometimes confusingly presented; and it is clearly not entirely watertight. But its radical economic conclusions are commonly reached with the aid of a respectable philosophical tradition. And the picture it offers of decision procedures under uncertainty is in many respects, I think, a reasonably convincing one.

But the picture is in some ways sombre. It portrays rather violent 'fluctuations in the market estimation of the marginal efficiency of different types of capital' (GT, p. 164) as endemic in the capitalist economy, since (if Keynes is right) they are a *natural* concomitant of behaviour that isn't unreasonable under ineradicable uncertainty. It's sensible, not foolish, action on the part of *rational* economic agents that is held to lead to the somewhat bizarre situation in which 'economic prosperity is excessively dependent on political and social atmosphere which is congenial to the average business man', with investment depending partly just on their 'nerves . . . digestions and reactions to the weather'. And it's because of this of course that Keynes himself draws a political moral in the concluding paragraph of chapter 12 of *The General Theory*, saying; 'I expect to see the State . . . taking an ever greater responsibility for directly organising investment'.[33]

---

[33] Not of course because the State has greater foresight or because it gains from institutionalised decision processes (it may lose) but rather because of its greater ability to press on with an investment programme whatever the state of confidence, with benefits to the stability of effective demand.

References

Bacharach, M. (1976), *Economics and the Theory of Games*, London: Macmillan.

Carabelli, A.M. (1988), *On Keynes' Method*, London: Macmillan.

Champernowne, D.G. (1969), *Uncertainty and Estimation in Economics*, Vol. 3, Oliver and Boyd.

Coates, J.M. (1990), 'Ordinary Language Economics: Keynes and the Cambridge Philosohers', PhD Dissertation, University of Cambridge.

Coddington, A. (1976), 'Keynesian Economics: the Search for First Principles', *Journal of Economic Literature*, XIV: 1258–73.

Goodman, N. (1954), *Fact, Fiction and Forecast*, Indianapolis, New York: The Bobbs-Merrill Company, Inc.

Hahn, F. and Hollis, M. (1979), *Philosophy and Economic Theory*, Oxford University Press.

Harrod, R.F. (1951), *The Life of John Maynard Keynes*, London: Macmillan.

Heiner, R.A. (1983), 'The Origin of Predictable Behaviour', *American Economic Review*, 73: 560–95.

Hollis, M. (1977), 'Rational Man and Social Science', mimeo.

Hume, D. (1938 edition, edited by Keynes and Sraffa), *An Abstract of a Treatise of Human Nature*, Cambridge University Press.

  (1739), *A Treatise of Human Nature*, Oxford University Press (references are to the edition edited by L.A. Selby-Bigge).

  (1948 edition), *Dialogues concerning Natural Religion*, Hafner.

  (1748), *Enquiries concerning the Human Understanding and concerning the Principles of Morals*, Oxford University Press (references are to the edition edited by L.A. Selby-Bigge).

Jeffreys, H. (1931), *Scientific Inference*, Cambridge University Press.

  (1948), *Theory of Probability* (2nd edition), Oxford University Press.

Keynes, J.M. (1921), *A Treatise on Probability*, London: Macmillan (references are to Vol. VIII of *The Collected Writings of John Maynard Keynes*, with its editorial foreword by R.B. Braithwaite).

  (1936), *The General Theory of Employment, Interest and Money*, London: Macmillan (references are to the Papermac edition).

  (1972, 1973), *The Collected Writings of John Maynard Keynes*, Vols. X and XIV, edited by D. Moggridge, London: Macmillan.

Lawson, T. (1985). Uncertainty and Economic Analysis', *Economic Journal*, 95: 909–27.

Lenz, J.W. (1958), 'Hume's Defense of Causal Inference', reprinted from the *Journal of the History of Ideas*, 19: 559–67, in V.C. Chappell (ed.) (1966), *Hume*, London: Macmillan.

Luce, R.D. and Raiffa, H. (1957), *Games and Decisions*, Wiley.

Minsky, H.P. (1975), *John Maynard Keynes*, Columbia University Press.

O'Donnell, R.M. (1989), *Keynes: Philosophy, Economics and Politics*, London: Macmillan.

Popkin, R.H. (1951), 'David Hume: His Pyrrhonism and His Critique of Pyrrhonism', reprinted from *The Philosophical Quarterly*, 1: 385–407, in V.C. Chappell (ed.) (1966), *Hume*, London: Macmillan.

Raz, J. (1975), *Practical Reason and Norms*, Hutchinson.

Runde, J. (1990). 'Keynesian Uncertainty and the Weight of Arguments', *Economics and Philosophy*, 6: 275–92.

Russell, B. (1912), *The Problems of Philosophy*, Oxford University Press (references are to the OPUS edition).

Shackle, G.L.S. (1967), *The Years of High Theory: Invention and Tradition in Economic Thought, 1926–1939*, Cambridge University Press.

Simon, H.A. (1976), 'From Substantive to Procedural Rationality'; reprinted in Hahn and Hollis (1979), 65–86.

Stove, D.C. (1965), 'Hume, Probability, and Induction', reprinted from the *Philosophical Review*. LXXIV, 160–177, in V.C. Chappell (ed.) (1966), *Hume*, London: Macmillan.

(1973), *Probability and Hume's Inductive Scepticism*, Oxford University Press.

Strawson, P.F. (1952), *Introduction to Logical Theory*, Methuen.

Von Mises, L. (1981), *Epistemological Problems of Economics*, trans. by G. Reisman, New York and London: New York University Press; first published 1933.